BODYSNATCHERS

Other books by the same author
The Murder Guide to London
The Crimes, Detection and Death of Jack the Ripper
Charles Dickens
Oscar Wilde
Rudyard Kipling
Shakespeare
The Social Novel in England (trans.)

BODYSNATCHERS

A History of
the Resurrectionists
1742–1832

Martin Fido

Weidenfeld and Nicolson
London

Illustration Acknowledgements

The photographs in this book are reproduced by permission
of the following: BBC Hulton Picture Library 1, 2, 3,
4 (below left and right), 5 (top left and below right),
6, 7 (top); The British Library 8; and The Mansell Collection
4 (top), 5 (top right and below left), 7 (below).

Published in Great Britain by
George Weidenfeld & Nicolson Limited
91 Clapham High Street
London SW4 7TA

ISBN 0 297 79393 4

Printed in Great Britain by Butler & Tanner Ltd
Frome and London

CONTENTS

ACKNOWLEDGEMENTS vii

1 The Origins of Bodysnatching in England.......................1
2 The Origins of Bodysnatching in Scotland 14
3 Helen Torrence and Jean Waldie 21
4 The Ben Crouch Gang 32
5 The Great Inflation 58
6 The Golden Age in Scotland 89
7 Burke and Hare 104
8 After Burke 132
9 The Bethnal Green Gang 140
10 Eliza Ross... 159
11 The End of Bodysnatching... 169

SOURCES... 173
INDEX.. 177

To the memory of Ben Crouch and John Hunter,
whose very different contributions to science should not have
been forgotten as they have by non-specialists.

ACKNOWLEDGEMENTS

The staffs of the British Library (Bloomsbury) and Newspaper Library (Colindale), the Greater London Archives, the Guildhall Library and the Public Record Office have been as helpful as ever. The Scottish National Record Office kindly sent me the trial papers of Helen Torrence and Jean Waldie.

I am exceedingly grateful to the Royal College of Surgeons and the Curator of the Hunterian Museum for letting me see the work of the greatest practical anatomist.

And to Nick Tregenza, who drew my attention to the item on Bentham in the *British Medical Journal*.

Heamoor/St Katharine by the Tower
1987

ONE

The Origins of Bodysnatching in England

Curiosity is innate in us. As children, we want to take things apart to see how they work.

A love of stability is also congenital. As adults we try to stop children's curiosity from destroying things.

These conflicting drives run through the history of anatomical research. Nothing is more interesting than ourselves, and nothing could seem more exciting than to know how we work. Yet nothing seems more deserving of respect and decorous treatment than the bodies of our friends and relatives. Pagan and Judaeo-Christian tradition alike insist upon reverent interment with religious rites for the preservation of that respect for humanity without which civilization must fall apart.

Galen, the first great anatomist (c. AD 130–200), circumvented the dilemma by dissecting animals – especially pigs and dogs – and assuming that what he found in them would be roughly duplicated in humans. His conclusions were impressive. He found that the arteries contained blood, and he postulated that internal organs all had specific purposes. But, naturally, his speculations about the human interior were imprecise.

Catholic Christendom was more concerned with the soul than the body, and based its philosophy firmly on the inviolable authority of tradition. It followed that Galen was not only unquestioned; it could be deemed heretical to question him. When curious philosophers insisted on making their own anatomical investigations, popes and emperors would give extremely rare permission for a servant to open up the body of an executed criminal while a doctor solemnly read from the works of Galen and pointed to the parts described. Where Galen's observations were quite at variance with the visible phenomena, it was simply asserted that the body now being examined was abnormal. Christendom was well set in the habit of discounting obvious truth when it conflicted with sanctified supposition.

Andreas Vesalius, the great Belgian anatomist (1514–64), finally undermined the supremacy of faith over fact. What he saw on dissecting bodies, he believed and described. And although the hostility of traditionalists led him to burn his books in despair, truth proved great and prevailed. Henceforth, anatomists would insist upon cutting up human corpses to find out the truth about human bodies and life, even though the Church burned Servetus in the hope that clerical superstitions might outlive his correct observation that blood passes from the heart into the lungs.

Vesalius set one other important precedent. Faced with social resistance to the mutilation of corpses, he acquired his first subject for serious dissection by theft. He stole the body of a malefactor hanging on a gibbet outside Louvain.

The trade of the bodysnatcher grew up when anatomy had proved its value in underpinning effective healing. Curious anatomical researchers might steal their own subjects. But as it became clear that a proper empirical understanding of the workings of the body made for more effective medicine than all the folklore, herbalism and traditional wisdom in existence, all surgical and medical students recognized a need to have seen inside a corpse before they tried to keep the living alive. The demand rose, and not all respectable professional men were willing to devote their nights to sneaking around gibbets and smuggling away dead pirates or highwaymen. The law was ineffective in resolving the conflict of tradition versus enquiry, which moved slowly at first in England.

In 1540 Henry VIII incorporated a dozen independent

surgeons with the Master Barbers of London, and the Company of Barber-Surgeons was chartered. A surgeon at that time did little but probe and dress wounds, amputate potentially gangrenous limbs, and bleed the sick for a variety of ailments. But the influence of continental research was making itself felt. The painters Leonardo and Michelangelo had found out so much about the muscular structure underlying body surfaces that the Pope prohibited them from entering hospitals, lest they start cutting up the living as well as the dead. And from the outset, the Company of Barber-Surgeons was granted the bodies of four felons a year for dissection at public lecture-demonstrations.

This was ample for the primitive Tudors. Surgeons were the crudest of medical men; socially and intellectually inferior to the learned physicians whose endless purgatives, mumbo-jumbo and general ignorance might cure by the placebo effect or poison by misadventure. Yet within a hundred years, Bacon had argued effectively for empiricism and Harvey had demonstrated the circulation of the blood. Surgeons were no longer content to be hairdressers and shavers whose possession of scissors and razors made them the obvious candidates to clean up external injury or amputate limbs. Some even knew that great advances were being made in Europe. In 1684 the surgeons petitioned unsuccessfully to be separated from the barbers.

Four years later William Cheselden was born. The father of English surgery was apprenticed to William Cowper, whose Fellowship of the Royal Society and discovery of the penile glands named after him indicate the intellectual interest he brought to chirurgeonry. Cheselden was more the practised healer than the anatomical investigator. He perfected lithotomy; the horrifying 'cutting for stone' which represented the sole internal surgical operation until the nineteenth century.

Stone in the bladder was a common and agonizing complaint. For the surgical cure, the patient was trussed like a chicken on his back with his wrists tied to his ankles. The surgeon probed the urethra with a catheter, following it by a broader probe to locate the stone. Then he made an incision through the perineum, and reaching into the bladder extracted the stone. There were no anaesthetics. The pain inflicted was appalling and many patients died under the operation. Cheselden's great success was that over half his patients survived. His humanity is indicated by two things. He often vomited *before* an operation, knowing both the torture he was about to inflict, and that he must not pause once he had begun. And one of his assistants was armed with a chronometer to make sure that he took no longer than three minutes operating.

Speed and determination were vital to the surgeon working before anaesthetics; his craft was little like the deliberate and delicate operating of our own day. As late as the 1820s, *The Lancet* savaged Bransby Cooper for taking fifty minutes over a lithotomy; a horrifying torture which killed the patient. Bransby's more competent uncle, Astley, rightly said that a surgeon must have the eye of an eagle, the hands of a lady and the heart of a lion. It was Astley who burst into tears when a child patient smiled confidently at him just as he was about to operate.

Three incidents in Cheselden's career were important to the future of bodysnatching. In the reign of Queen Anne he started to give private anatomy classes at his house in Cheapside. For these, he bought the bodies of executed felons from the scaffold. And in 1714 the Company put a stop to this independent educational venture. Their Court record stated:

> Our Master acquainted the Court that Mr. Wm. Cheselden, a member of the Company did frequently procure the dead bodies of malefactors from the place of execution and dissect the same at his own house as well during the Company's publick lectures as at other times without the word of the Governors and contrary to the Company's By-Law in that behalf by which means it becomes more difficult for the beadles to bring away the Company's bodies and likewise drew away the members from the publick lectures and dissections at the Hall.

Ten years later Jonathan Wild was executed. The 'thief-taker-general', whose Lost Property Office succeeded because he also controlled most of London's robbers and cut-

4

purses, was smuggled away from the gallows by his friends and buried at dead of night. Already they feared that 'the surgeons' would want his body. And they were right. It was dug up and delivered to them, and his skeleton may be seen today in the Hunterian Museum at the Royal College of Surgeons. Cheselden had identified a need for more than four anatomy demonstrations a year, and pin-pointed a problem in the insufficiency of subjects obtainable direct from the gallows.

In 1731, Cheselden's activities closed another potential research area. He had been appointed surgeon to Queen Caroline, and was anxious to find a cure for her deafness. To this end he negotiated to secure the living body of a convicted criminal named Rey. Rey was reprieved on condition that Cheselden deafened him and experimented on his eardrums to find out whether perforation would be of value to the Queen. There was a public outcry. How, asked the laity, could making one man deaf help another woman hear? The *cognoscenti* replied that the same objection had been made to experimental operations on the eye, yet these meant that Cheselden could now remove cataracts.

The Hanoverian hangers-and-floggers had a more profound objection. No mere royal surgeon should cheat the gallows of its prey. And suppose Rey escaped from custody while under Cheselden's care?

The authorities yielded to the pressure. While they honourably insisted that Rey's reprieve had been promised, and it stood, they prohibited Cheselden from experimenting. Human vivisection was thenceforth barred, and only a miniscule section of the German medical profession in the 1940s has ever attempted to revive it. Anatomical research is essentially practised on cadavers.

In 1745 Cheselden was a leading figure in the negotiations which led to the establishment of a separate Company of Surgeons, with its Hall in Old Bailey, conveniently next door to Newgate where subjects awaited execution. With the jealous barber-bleeders excluded, and Cheselden Master of the Company in 1746, the door was open for legitimate private anatomy schools.

William Hunter, a young Scot who combined a growing

practice as a 'male-midwife' (obstetrician) with running the anatomical museum he had inherited from his deceased fiancée's father, seized the opportunity. He had studied anatomy under Frank Nicholls of Lincoln's Inn Fields, whose 'corrosive method' entailed exposition from wax models made by injecting veins and arteries, and then dissolving the human tissue in acid. He used no more than two cadavers for a course of thirty-nine lectures, and Hunter complained that 'all was harangue ; very little was seen'.

Hunter now started courses on 'the Paris model', where each student was assured of putting his own knife into a body. In Paris, this was achieved by the authorities' giving the surgeons executed felons' bodies and all stillborn infants from hospitals. Hunter had to send his assistants to rob graves, and they in turn had to bribe sextons and porters to help them. The trade of bodysnatching had emerged.

It was given instant prestige by the patronage of Hunter's younger brother John. Pretty much the fool of a large Scottish family, John had been an undistinguished schoolboy, became a cabinet-maker, and on his master's failure, wrote to brother William to see if there might be employment for him in London. William, academically brilliant and socially on the make, decided that he could use his brother as a lab assistant, and so brought to London the towering genius of English comparative anatomy.

For John proved more than a skilful carver of bodies. He was intensely curious about the whole nature of life. And being utterly unbookish, he went direct to life for his study. He asked simple but vital questions (How can a heavier-than-air bird glide through the air?) and found answers by dissection and observation (its bones contain air sacs). He passionately dissected every animal, rare or common, he could lay hands on. He was the first person to articulate an elephant's skeleton. Yet he used the household sparrow to demonstrate important features of the male gonads. His demonstration preparations (hundreds of which survive) have the craftsmanship of eighteenth century violins, and the imaginative breadth, profundity and harmony of Mozart quintets. He assembled a massive collection of over 14,000 specimens and preparations to give ocular demonstration of the nature and relations of animal organisms. Severely diminished by enemy action, his collection has been restored and augmented, and represents one of the supremely great achievements of human intelligence and creativity. Darwin's central perception of the unity of life is instantly apparent in this work. Compared with the creative scientist Hunter, Darwin seems merely a natural philosopher who thought out one central aspect of his predecessor's great insight, and sometimes used rather suspect written authorities to support his case.

This overwhelming, and grotesquely underrated genius, happily retained the common touch of the Scottish country cabinet-maker, even as he rose to surgical eminence and headed the anatomy department at St George's Hospital. His vulgar tastes were quietly deplored by his brother: John greatly enjoyed the theatre, and loved to join in the noise made by the gallery. He also thoroughly enjoyed the company of bodysnatchers who, indeed, have been blamed by some of his genteel biographers for coarsening his tastes.

Unfortunately we know nothing of his association with them except that it was noted by contemporaries. There are varying accounts of his acquisition of one of his prize exhibits: the skeleton of Charles Byrne 'the Irish giant'. This depressive 23-year-old alcoholic claimed to be eight feet two inches tall, and may (with cartilage) have touched eight foot. (His skeleton now stands seven feet eight inches.) He knew the surgeons coveted his unusual body, and made arrangements to foil them, either paying fishermen or arranging with friends for his burial at sea in a lead coffin. Hunter either reimbursed the fishermen, or yielded to the increasing extortion of the friends. In any case, he paid the amazing sum of £500 (several thousand pounds of today's money) for the body, which he hastily boiled at his Earl's Court home, exhibiting the skeleton after it had been articulated. This lavish expenditure on his science was typical. He devoted all his resources to the collection, and must have kept several bodysnatchers in comfort, supplying the many subjects he needed for the comparative demonstration of variant forms of organs, joints and teeth.

Nor did William Hunter allow this trade to dwindle. In

1767 he bought a large house in Great Windmill Street for his home and dissecting academy. Here, for the next sixty years, bodysnatchers delivered corpses in hampers to be left inside the railings, which can still be seen at the old façade, next to the former Windmill Theatre. As William concentrated increasingly on obstetrics, he specialized in the collection of female corpses in various stages of pregnancy, until he had dissected between 300 and 400. With this massive basis of practical observation, his published masterpiece on the gravid uterus took twenty-three years to complete, and deservedly stood as the first authority on the subject for over a hundred years.

Not one of William's gravid wombs could have come through official channels, since pregnant women were never hung. So many other felons were, however, that even the hanging lobby wondered whether there was not some disproportion in having the same penalty for stealing a sheep or a lamb, or killing the shepherd while you were at it! Rather than reduce the law's severity, the Act of 1752 to Prevent the Horrid Crime of Murder stipulated that convicted murderers should be executed the day after they were sentenced (unless that day should be Sunday); that at the discretion of the court, their bodies should then be given to the surgeons for dissection and exhibition to the public; that they should not receive Christian burial, and unlike other convicted felons, they should not have the funeral service read over them as they travelled to Tyburn. The primary (and blasphemous) aim was to reduce their hope of salvation, by restricting their chance of repentance and refusing the Church's blessing. A secondary advantage should be the provision of bodies for science.

The secondary aim failed completely. There simply were not enough convicted felons – let alone murderers – to meet the anatomists' needs. Between 1749 and 1756, there were only 306 hangings in London and Middlesex. After the Act of 1752, the surgeons could anticipate receiving about ten or thirteen cadavers a year from the courts. The Hunters' research alone required more than ten times that amount, and none of William's could be executed.

The new legal penalty of dissection had various consequences. Criminals undoubtedly feared it; not so much because they might be damningly dismembered when required to rise again on the Day of Judgment, as because hanging by strangulation was not necessarily instantly lethal. They dreaded coming round from a death-like coma to find a surgeon's knife burrowing into their entrails, as happened to a rather nasty sixteen-year-old rapist named William Duitt.

The general public formed the impression that dissection was the well-earned penalty for the worst of crimes. The example of the ribald rationalist wit, Dr Messenger Mounsey, did not catch on, when he left his 95-year-old body for dissection in 1788 with caustic observations on the pointlessness of Christian burial.

Surgeons' Hall had skeletons in niches as its macabre ornamentation, and these were known to have come from such villains as Jonathan Wild, or the horrible Restoration 'badger game' murderers, Country Tom and Canbery Bess. When exposure of murderers' corpses in the Hall was formalized in 1766, the public would see these remains at the same time as they came to witness the notorious killers who were about to join them: Mrs Brownrigg the servant-murderer in 1768, Dr Levy Weill the lethal housebreaker in 1772, and Hogan the mulatto in 1786.

The last revealed another objection to the penalty. Naked corpses attracted lascivious spectators. Hogan had killed and robbed a servant-girl who resisted his forceful advances, and was ultimately taken in bed with another girl friend. *The Times* was deeply shocked that his reputation and race interested those who hoped that he might be unusually well endowed. 'The numbers of women, who daily *unsex* themselves to see the remains of this atrocious criminal are uncommonly great,' it complained.

The occasional exhibitions and dissections at Surgeons' Hall were not the primary source of anatomical education. John Hunter gave lectures at St George's which were sparsely but selectly attended by men who realized that, despite his poor delivery, they were in the presence of a great genius, and went on to become the leading surgeons and anatomists of the next generation. William and his assistants, Sheldon, Cruikshank and Baillie gave classes at Windmill Street which were attended by the majority of students from St George's and the Westminster Hospital. St Bartholomew's and the London Hospital began teaching anatomy, as did Guy's and St Thomas's jointly as the United Borough Hospitals. And a new private dissecting academy opened in Thavies Inn in 1780, run by William Marshall.

He was no outstanding anatomist: John Hunter put him down severely when he claimed that he had always observed deformation in the dissected brains of lunatics. Nor was he a great lecturer. His classes were attended because he provided so many excellent subjects for dissection.

In 1785 this posed a problem for the authorities. Two excisemen saw five men in black followed by a porter bearing a large hamper pass St Andrew's church, Holborn, between 8.00 and 9.00 p.m. on Friday 14 October. Suspecting contraband, they followed the party to Marshall's house in Thavies Inn and demanded admission. The men in black, and another man from upstairs, assured them that the hamper contained 'goods for the Faculty'. When the officers felt inside it, and thought they found meat, the men said that it was pork from the country. But the officers quickly exposed four infants' bodies.

The men in black were gentlemen. Mere labourers and sextons could be flogged at the cart's tail from Kingsgate Street to Dyott Street and back, as happened to John Holmes and Peter Williams with their accomplice Esther Donaldson when they were caught with the body of Mrs Jane Sainsbury, extracted from St George's churchyard, Bloomsbury, where Holmes and Williams worked. But gentlemen were never exposed to such penalties. The authorities grumbled about Marshall and his men, but did nothing.

It was not until 1788 that the law took firm cognizance of the undesirability of surgeons' robbing graves. Then, in *R.v.Lynn* the whole question was thrashed out. Mr Lynn, a south London surgeon, was charged at the Court of King's Bench with taking a female body from St Saviour's churchyard for the purposes of dissection. His counsel protested that there was no case to answer. 'There was a peculiar silence in all law books with regard to the rights that belonged to the body,' he noted. It was no living person's property and so it could not be stolen. It was not a subject of the crown with duties, and so it had no rights of its own. Punishments for disinterment in the past had always related to the purpose – usually witchcraft, or exhibition in the streets to the detriment of public order. Here the purpose was the legitimate, laudable and necessary intention of advancing the science of healing.

The prosecution riposted with a case in which a surgeon had been fined for preventing Christian burial. But that could not apply to Lynn who had disinterred his subject after burial.

From the bench, Lord Kenyon happily misremembered a precedent. He believed that bodies, including the High Tory bigot Dr Sacheverell's, had been stolen from St Andrew's churchyard in 1744, and the malefactors punished. Nobody else in court knew anything about this, and so the fact that he was quite mistaken was overlooked. (The actual offence was the theft of lead coffins, including Sacheverell's.) With a 'precedent' to support them, the judges were happy to concur that disturbing a grave was obviously an offence in common law, and certainly liable to cause a breach of the peace. Lynn was told that he might not have known his act was criminal, and so he was leniently fined £10. But the surgical profession had been warned. From now on, the 'gentlemen in black' would not do their own grave-robbing. The field was clear for a specialist profession.

Moreover, the authorities could make arrests with the confident anticipation of convictions. As there was still no theft of property involved, bodysnatching was a mis-demeanour and not a felony (as long as the coffin and graveclothes were properly returned to the desecrated tomb!). But this could still entail several months' imprison-ment, and surgeons were not going to risk that.

The problems surgeons encountered under this prohibition are well outlined in a letter William Hamilton sent home while he was a student at Great Windmill Street.

> The Dr. [i.e. Hunter] is particularly hurried this week as he is afraid his body won't keep .... Bodies are vastly scarce at present. Some of the men have been taken up and tried but I hope this will soon be over.

And again:

> Bodies are vastly scarce two resurrection men are taken up
> and all the burying ground is watched so that I am afraid
> we shall have little dissecting for some time there is nothing
> but an arm and my leg in the dissecting room at present.

The term 'resurrection man' seems to have been invented
by a Southwark bodysnatcher to describe his occupation in
the 1770s. They were also sometimes called 'sack-'em-up'
men, from their practice of bundling cadavers into sacks for
transportation from cemeteries. But none of these terms was
familiar to the general public during the eighteenth century.

In 1792 Marshall had another brush with the law. He was
taken before the Guildhall magistrates, charged with having
two bodies in his possession. Fortunately for him, the
magistrates declined to find him guilty of any offence, though
the undertaker who had supplied him was convicted. The law
had now put itself into the illogical and immoral position
achieved by American Prohibition of alcohol, and most
countries' harassment of prostitution. The purveyor was a
criminal. The customer was not. The inevitable consequence
was that the goods became more expensive; more people
were attracted into the hazardous but lucrative business of
supplying; and the repressive law strengthened the trade.

At some time in the late 1790s, Ben Crouch and Jack
Harnett probably joined Jack's uncle Bill in bodysnatching,
though their heyday came ten to twenty years later. John
'Lousy Jack' Parker was the most notorious bodysnatcher of
the last years of the eighteenth century. Many parishes had
detainers out for him when, in 1797, he was finally arrested in
Blackman Street, Southwark, carrying the sacked-up body of
Sarah Suny from Newington churchyard. He was ferociously
sentenced to two years hard labour in St George's Fields
House of Correction; eloquent testimony to the authorities'
growing impatience with bodysnatching.

Marshall gave up his academy in 1800. The reason was not
the law, but a narrowing of the profession. The Company of
Surgeons yearned for the distinction achieved by their
Scottish and Irish counterparts, where Edinburgh and Dublin
boasted Royal Colleges of Surgeons. They succeeded in

gaining a Royal Collegiate Charter, and proceeded to try and enforce a closed shop of their own licensees. Headed by Baillie and Cruikshank at Great Windmill Street, Henry Cline and Astley Cooper at the United Borough Hospitals and John Abernethy at St Bartholomew's, the successors of the great Hunter brothers tried to make sure that no more penniless woodworkers might come down from Scotland and revolutionize science without benefit of Latin and a college education. Marshall withdrew cautiously into private practice. The surgeons were laying the ground for a great upsurge in bodysnatching, by introducing competition between private schools and hospitals.

TWO

The Origins of
Bodysnatching in Scotland

Surgery, anatomy and bodysnatching all show clearly that
Scotland is no provincial sector of Britain, but a nation with
its own advanced cultural, legal and educational heritage,
quite apart from England's.

Thirty-five years before Henry VIII granted the London
Barber-Surgeons their four annual felons, the Edinburgh
Barber-Surgeons had petitioned the Town Council:

> ... that we may have anis in the year ane condampnit man
> after he be deid, to make anatomea of, quairthrow we may
> heif experience, ilk ane to instruct utheris, and we sall do
> suffrage for the soule.

Nineteen years before Cheselden fell foul of the London
Company of Barber-Surgeons by hijacking their malefactors'
bodies, Alexander Monteith's private academy had been
granted 'of those bodies that dye in the correction-house and
of the bodies of foundlings that dye upon the breast', while
the Scottish Barber-Surgeons were compensatorily granted:

> ... the bodies of foundlings who dye betwixt the time that
> they are weaned and their being put to schools or trades;
> also the dead bodies of such as are stiflet in the birth, which
> are exposed, and have none to owne them; as also the dead

14

bodies of such as are felo de se, and have none to owne them, likeways the bodies of such as are put to death by sentence of the magistrate, and have none to owne them.

This was coming close to the continental practice whereby effectively all unclaimed bodies went to science. And Scotland's sympathetic attitude to anatomy extended beyond the capital and the rival metropolis of Glasgow. In 1636, William Gordon of King's College, Aberdeen, received from the Privy Council an annual grant of:

... twa bodies of men, being notable malefactors, executte in thair bounds, especiallie being rebells and outlawis; and failzeing of them, the bodies of the poorer sort, dieing in hospitals; or abortive bairns, foundlings; or of those of no qualitie, who has died of thare diseases and has few friends or acquaintance that can tak exception.

Startlingly unsqueamish in their class bias, the councillors were also evidently determined to encourage medicine in all Scottish universities.

In Edinburgh this produced the great dynasty of Alexander Monros: father, son and grandson each successively holding the Chair of Anatomy and Surgery. Alexander Monro I (1697–1767) studied in Edinburgh and London (where Cheselden directed his dissection), and then in Paris and Leyden. In 1719 he returned to Edinburgh as Professor of Anatomy and Surgery to the Surgeons' College, and opened dissecting rooms in Surgeon's Square. In 1720 he became the university's first Professor of Anatomy, a post he yielded to his son in 1764.

Alexander Monro II (1733–1817) was the best scientist of the three. He trained in Edinburgh, London (under William Hunter), Paris, Leyden and Berlin. In 1755 he became Professor of Anatomy and Surgery, coadjutant to his father. In 1770 he beat off an attempt to divide his post into separate chairs of anatomy and surgery, and in 1808 he retired, handing over the undivided empire to Alexander Monro III.

The last of the Monros (1773–1859) was not a worthy heir to the great medical faculty they had established. His work was derivative from theirs: his lecture notes were, reputedly, theirs, in such unaltered condition that ninteenth century students delightedly awaited the annual occasion when he would follow his grandfather in remarking, 'When I was at Leyden in 1715 . . . .' But the tradition of Monros at Edinburgh seemed lustrous, and Humphry Davy was among those who came to hear Alexander Monro III lecture.

And the Edinburgh centre of learning affected the entire kingdom. William Cullen, who trained there, became a country doctor and, as such, inspired the young William Hunter to pursue medical research before himself becoming Professor of Chemistry and Physic, first at Glasgow and then at Edinburgh. It escaped nobody's attention that many of the great surgeons of London were Scots: both Hunters, William Cruikshank, and later Robert Liston.

Scottish comparative anatomy was carried forward by John Barclay (1758–1826), whose early training for the ministry proved a false start. His rural parishioners found him unduly eccentric, given his extraordinary habit of dissecting toads. After qualifying in medicine at Edinburgh, Barclay opened a private dissecting academy in Surgeon's Square, which attracted the brightest and best of the capital's students once they were able to compare his inspiring independent research with Alexander Monro III's hack-work.

Scottish students, indeed, were and are more vociferously receptive to good teaching than their English counterparts. The medics among them were determined to follow through the practical suggestions put before them in anatomy classes. While the first two Monros were generally content to stay within the law and only used the cadavers they had been granted, this meant that they were constantly fishing out heavily worked-over pieces of flesh from buckets of brine, and hoping that their students would be able to detect the former paths of nerves and arteries incised in them. The students were not satisfied, and sought their own cadavers to see the structures clearly for themselves. Thus they themselves became the bodysnatchers of Scotland.

Disinterment touched a raw nerve in Scottish sensitivity. As early as the great witch-trials of 1590–1 it was clear that the authorities morbidly dreaded the notion of corpse-robbing. The witches' confessions, especially the important evidence of Agnes Sampson, 'the wise wife of Nether Keith', were transparently coerced responses to predetermined questions. The Devil's alleged insistence that his Scottish followers must memorize his profound hatred for the King as an exceptionally good man and a close friend of God obviously derived more from diabolical tortures inflicted by the King's inquisitors than from any real Satanic celebrations.

And we may reasonably infer that their obsessions also inspired Mistress Sampson's unlikely confession to :

> . . . hir develisch practesis, and namelie [especially] of hir passing to Natoun Kirk under nycht, with the witch of Cabanie and vtheris ; and thair taking vp the bwreit [buried] people and junting of thame [taking away their limbs] quhairof scho maid inchantit powder for Wichcraft.

This didn't even convince the jury, so a description of a more elaborate coven at North Berwick was racked out of Mistress Sampson. Here the Devil 'like ane mekle blak man' took a roll-call of a hundred followers, and then :

> One his command, thay opnit vp the graves, twa within and ane without the kirk, and tuik of the jountis of thair fingaris, tais and neise, and partit thame amangis thame : and the said Agnes Sampsoun gatt for hir pairt, ane windene scheit [winding sheet] and twa jountis . . . . The Devill commandit thame to keip the jountis vpon thame, to do evill withall.

Such an obsession with imaginary bodysnatching fore-shadowed a considerable role for resurrectionism when surgery made the real thing desirable.

In 1711, even before Alexander Monro's appointment, student raids on Greyfriar's churchyard produced protests in Edinburgh. In the face of a long satirical poem in heroic couplets attacking this sacrilege, the surgeons piously denied all responsibility.

In 1725, Edinburgh citizens rioted in protest against the surgical students' depredations. Alexander Monro I took fright, and moved his dissecting equipment and specimens from Surgeon's Square to the security of the university.

The previous year there was an outrage at Musselburgh. A

woman had been hanged, and her relatives were determined to give her Christian burial. A party of students was equally determined to seize the corpse for dissection. A savage free fight took place over the body, when it suddenly revived and disappointed both factions. For thirty years she lived on, known as 'Half-hangit Maggie Dickson'.

By 1742 there is evidence that student bodysnatchers were being supported by some professional purveyors. At the same time the term 'Resurrection' makes its first ironical appearance in an account of bodysnatching. A long piece of doggerel entitled *Groans from the Grave: or, A Melancholy Account of the New Resurrection, practised in and about Edinburgh* reveals that two gardeners named Samuel and Richardson had been digging up bodies at Potterow and Westkirk; an accomplice called Haddon had organized their sale; and one Cochran had arranged transport of bodies from Inverask, Musselburgh and Fisherow. Beadles at Westkirk and Libertoun were dismissed for accepting bribes from the resurrectionists, and Haddon's house, nicknamed 'Resurrection Hall', was sacked by the mob, which burned all his furniture and set their women to scrape the plaster off the walls.

The poet seems to show cautious respect for the learned professors and maybe students of the university, and casts the blame for bodysnatching on the reckless surgeons' apprentices:

> We need not here *Edinburgh's* College blame,
> Nor on the Sons of Learning lay the same,
> Their Principles is surely more refin'd,
> Virtue's in them, they're to no Vice inclin'd.
> Good reason Malefactors given should be,
> To try the Art of brave Anatomie,
> Or Persons that deprive themselves of Life,
> Fit for nought but th'anatomizing Knife.
> But Persons of an honest reputation,
> Who lifts the same, merits his own Damnation.
> 'Tis only airy, flory Surgeon Lads,
> Intoxicate with Wine, debauch'd with Bauds,
> Hastens to some remote Country Church-yard,
> The Beadle gets, gives him a large reward

Hires a Trone-man, sometimes gets a chair,
And in short Time they compass their desire.

The writing is not good enough for one to be sure whether
sarcasm is intended or not in the praise of 'Edinburgh's
College'. It would certainly become one of the known
differences between Edinburgh and Glasgow that the latter
deliberately left its students to find their own subjects for
dissection, so that student bodysnatchers kept prices low.
Whereas Edinburgh University insisted that the professors
would supply cadavers. And since they could not carry out all
their own sacking-up (though some young surgeons did a
great deal, and one great surgeon would also become one of
the greatest nineteenth century resurrectionists) they had
recourse to hired diggers and porters as well as students, and
prices were concomitantly higher. There was a minor wrangle
between the two universities as to whether Glasgow's system
was preferable as it assisted poor students and gave a sort of
character training, or Edinburgh's was the better as it allowed
genteel students to keep their hands clean. In either case,
doctors and students were sufficiently involved that the
authorities were extremely chary of bringing Scottish bodysnatchers to court.

Further afield there was no alternative to students finding
their own subjects. The Aberdeen Medico-Chirurgical
Society, founded in 1789, was to all intents and purposes a
bodysnatching organization with a largely student membership and committee. In 1801 its secretary was bound over in
his father's surety of £50 for stealing the body of James Marr
from Spittal churchyard. And five years later, the secretary
was deploying all his tact in letters to the authorities, offering
to defray the expenses of re-interring a cadaver found by the
watch in the society's rooms; tipping the constables for their
'genteel behaviour on the occasion'; and sending a guinea for
the widow 'to stop her clamour'. High-handed insensitivity
toward the feelings of the bereaved poor is pretty consistently
evinced by Scottish medics of the bodysnatching period, and
ultimately made it very difficult for the surgeons to win the
legislative help they needed.

Since the authorities were unwilling to act firmly against

bodysnatching, citizens had to organize their own protection of their dead. Watchmen were hired, or relatives would take turns to sleep in specially constructd watchhouses at cemeteries. The most elaborate of these had gun-ports and alarm bells. Watchmen would shoot at anything that moved; once they killed a pig near Aberdeen.

Mortsafes were a peculiarly Scottish device. These were heavy iron cages erected over graves and firmly embedded in the soil. They were a most effective means of inhibiting disinterment, and thrifty owners used a block and tackle mounted on three sheer-legs to hoist them out of place and use them over again on new graves when necessary.

The Quakers of Kinmuck were thriftier still. They made a stout cage of wrought iron in two halves which could be bolted around the coffin and buried with it. When the body was deemed to have putrefied beyond being any use for the surgeons, the coffin was dug up, the portable mortsafe was unlocked and taken back to the Meeting House, and there it waited for the next Friend's death. It did at least mean that the poorest member of Kinmuck Preparative Meeting was assured of resting in peace.

THREE

Helen Torrence And Jean Waldie

Professional bodysnatching was hardly ten years old when two Edinburgh women hit upon an economical alternative to traditional sacking-up. Sir Walter Scott, whose recapitulation of their case seems indebted to courtroom gossip rather than trial papers, described them as 'two resurrection-women'. In fact, big Helen Torrence was a needlewoman, while little Jean Waldie kept house for her husband, and sick-nursed. But in the summer of 1751 Helen Torrence certainly offered a physician's apprentice a cadaver.

The season was ill-chosen. Dr Russell's other apprentices were away, and eighteen-year old James Flint was unwilling to accept it on his own. But as autumn passed and his comrades came back to work, he began to regret having missed the opportunity, and in November Mistress Torrence played on his regrets.

She came to Dr Russell's shop to have sores on her leg dressed. Flint conferred with his fellow-apprentice, James Arthur, and the two offered to cure Helen's leg if she would obtain them a body. Helen returned on Friday 29 November saying that she would have one the next day. Her neighbour, Jean Waldie, was to sit up with a dead boy that night, and while his father slept the two women proposed to bribe the mother to release the body to them and weight the coffin with something else.

This offer was over-optimistic. Helen had suggested to Jean that it would be very profitable for them *if* their friend Janet Johnston Dallas's little boy John were to die. John was eight, and had been grievously afflicted with scrofula for the past four years. The tubercular infection had robbed him of speech and hearing, produced sores and restricted his movements so that he was unable to leave his parents' house. But unknown to the would-be resurrection-women his condition was improving. He was starting to recover his hearing, and was able to visit neighbours on his family's staircase and indicate his needs by sign-language.

What Jean and Helen assessed correctly was John's parents' relative dispositions. John Dallas senior, a sedan-chair porter, was a vehement man who tolerated no family or outside interference with his convenience. Janet Johnston by contrast (working-class Edinburgh women still used their maiden names after marriage) was easily manipulated by the promise of a dram. She was 'a puir drunken body', according to Jean Waldie.

Late at night on Saturday 30 November, Flint and Arthur went to tiny Fairlie's Close where Helen Torrence lived in a tenement, with Jean Waldie and her husband John Fair immediately above her, and alewife Nellie Fraser below. They were disappointed. No subject awaited them, and Helen Torrence regretted that the mother had refused. But she was in hopes of finding another that night, and sent Jean Waldie out to pretend to look for it. After two hours the apprentices were restless, and Helen went to see what had become of her partner. She returned to say that there would be no body that night, but urged the young men to return the following day.

The next day was the sabbath, and the boys did not break it by going out to buy their subject. At 10.00 p.m., however, Jean Waldie came to their rooms at Dr Russell's shop with the exciting news that she had acquired a body. It was at home in her drawers, she said, adding that she dared not carry it away at present as she was suspected of stealing it. She would have to leave town for a couple of days, and she successfully scrounged a shilling off them for her travelling expenses to Musselburgh or Dalkeith.

By Monday the apprentices were suspicious. They went

over to Helen Torrence's, 'to see', as James Arthur said, 'whether the women were biteing them or if there was really a subject'. Helen assured them that there was one, but Jean had locked it in her rooms and gone to the country taking her key with her.

Next day, Janet Johnston went to visit Helen Torrence bearing a piece of linen. She wanted a shirt made for her younger son Charles, and Helen promised that it would be ready that night. Soon after Mistress Johnston had left, Flint and Arthur arrived to try stronger measures to discover the truth. They bought Mistress Torrence a pint of ale, and, as they hoped, this unlocked her tongue. She confessed that there was no body, but promised that there really would be one soon. When they left, it was time for earnest conference with Mistress Waldie, whose precipitate acceptance of expenses made the acquisition of a subject urgent rather than desirable. Needlesss to say, there had been no visit to Dalkeith or Musselburgh, and it is a safe bet that the shilling had been turned into drams of whisky and pints of ale.

Now came Helen Torrence's insinuating suggestion that it would be a good idea to take John Dallas away from his home . . . and he would probably be dead before he reached Fairlie's Close.

Around six o'clock the two women were drinking ale together when Mrs Johnston came to collect Charles's shirt. The button-holes in the neck were still to do, she was told, and it would take about half an hour. Why not stop and share the beer with them? Mrs Johnston willingly acquiesced.

Jean Waldie complained that she had been feeling colicky all day and really must retire to bed. At Helen Torrence's bidding, Mrs Johnston took a candle and a pint of ale, and saw her upstairs. Not that Mistress Waldie was too sick to forego a tonic. She and Janet had not quite enough for a dram, so Janet went back downstairs, took a contribution of a ha'penny from big Helen, and saw Jean Waldie comfortable.

As Janet and Helen enjoyed their share of the dram downstairs, they heard a footstep on the landing, followed by a signal knock on the floor above. Helen Torrence immediately went up to see what Jean wanted, and after a little came back to tell Janet that Jean's husband John Fair had come home and

ordered another bottle of ale for his wife's colic. Janet and
Helen went down to Nellie Fraser's to fetch it. Helen settled
Janet comfortably in the alewife's cramped parlour with
another pint while she took the bottle up; returned to say
that John Fair was looking after his wife; and went out again
with yet another pint of ale. This time she was away for at
least half an hour, and explained her absence by saying her
child had woken up and she had to give it suck.

But, in fact, she went quickly over to Stonielaw's Close,
where the Dallases lived, to find out whether their neighbours
were up and about and likely to observe any kidnapping of
young John. It is unlikely that John Fair had come home at
all, as his presence would have put paid to the next phase of
the plan.

By Jean Waldie's own account, when she learned it was all
clear, she rose quickly from her sickbed and made her way to
Stonielaw's Close, where she found John alone, looking over
the window-sill. She persuaded him to come out with her . . .
and somehow he was dead by the time she reached Fairlie's
Close. She laid him down on her chest of drawers, and
hurried to Dr Russell's to tell the apprentices to come quickly
and remove their subject before her husband came home from
work and made trouble.

Janet Johnston, meanwhile, was happily drinking the early
evening away with Helen Torrence and Nellie Fraser. At
about eight o'clock there were footsteps outside, and Helen
went quickly to the door.

'Gentlemen,' she said, 'will ye come in and give us a
dram?'

But Nellie Fraser interrupted. There were to be no men in
her house that night.

This led Janet to think of the time, and she hurried away to
Gilbert Gow's the vintner's where she expected to find her
husband enjoying a drink. She was too late. He was at that
moment coming into Stonielaw's Close with his five-year-old
son Charles, and was very angry to find his wife and elder son
missing. Janet cautiously took a can of water from Gow's and
made her way back home.

She encountered the furious chairman on the stairs asking
where she had been and where little John was. She assured

him she had only been out for half an hour (she had been at least two and a half!) fetching water from the well, and John was upstairs in their room. He was not, of course, as she soon discovered. Her irate husband seized hold of her and kicked her all the way down the stairs again, telling her not to come back until she had found John. Janet asked around the house for her son, and went in to a neighbour's where she stayed until 10.00 p.m.

Meanwhile the anatomy trade was proceeding briskly. Jean Waldie found Andrew Anderson, another medical student, with Flint and Arthur. Unlike Russell's apprentices, he had private lodgings where he could hide the subject, and he went with them back to Fairlie's Close. There he went upstairs and saw the body of a young boy, clothed only in a shirt, lying on the chest of drawers. Rigor mortis had not yet set in, but Anderson detected no warmth, and was not suspicious of anything but natural death. He returned to Helen Torrence's room and the bargaining proceeded. Would two shillings be enough, the students enquired? Both women protested to heaven that they had been at far more expense than that to procure the subject. They were satisfied, though, with ten pence for immediate alcoholic sustenance, and the two shillings as a deposit towards an ultimate total of five.

There remained the question of transportation. John was too large to be concealed under Anderson's greatcoat, so the students asked if the women could carry it for them. This was a job for big Helen who wrapped the body in her apron and lugged it through the streets to Anderson's room where the boys hid it under the bed. For this porterage, which kept her out till after 10.00 p.m., she was immediately paid another sixpence.

John Dallas went to bed with Charles, bolting his door against his wife. He ignored her timid knock at ten o'clock, and so Janet betook herself to Fairlie's Close.

There she was surprised to find Jean Waldie alone, out of bed, and sitting by the fire in Helen Torrence's room. Jean's battered shoes and bare legs were filthy with street-dirt to the knees. How had she come by that, Janet wondered?

'That's my business', snapped Jean.

And where was Helen?

'She'll be back soon.'

Which she was. Instead of explaining her absence she offered Janet the glad news that Dr Russell's servant had dropped in earlier and given them a dram. She and Jean had taken all they wanted of it, and Janet might have the rest.

Janet did so.

Then the women sent out for yet more ale, which they all enjoyed, while Helen's daughter brought in a tub of water for Jean to wash her feet.

'Ye did ill,' Janet told them, 'to keep me so long. My husband has turned me out.'

'No matter,' replied Helen. 'You can lie with me all night.'

And so she did! Moreover Jean Waldie refused to go to her own room again, saying she would lie by the fireplace in her clothes. So both these evil women slept peacefully with their innocent gull.

During the night Jean crept into bed beside Helen who was lying head to tail with her guest. Helen woke up and asked her why she did so. After a little murmuring, Jean went away to her own room.

In the small hours, Helen Torrence woke again, and felt under her pillow for some snuff. Her pockets were not where she had left them. (These were bags on draw-strings, which women wore over their petticoats.) A little searching discovered them pushed against the wall beside the bed. Helen examined them, and Janet Johnston woke up to hear her cursing that two of three sixpences she had left in them were missing. Janet offered to let Helen search her, but her hostess assured her that it was not necessary; she knew well that Jean had taken them. The two women went back to sleep.

In the morning Helen went upstairs to have it out with her thieving partner. When she returned, Jean followed her and threw sixpence at her, shouting that it was half hers, anyway. Why had she said that, Janet wondered? Helen's explanation was that the eighteen pence had been given her by John Fair for an apron and a handkerchief for his wife.

Janet took leave of her hostess, and went back to Stonielaw's Close where her husband still refused to let her in. Since she had stayed out all night, he shouted, she could go back to whoever she had been with. He would look after

Charles for the future, and she could take care of little John. Janet made desultory enquiries for her son in the neighbour-hood, and then went back to Fairlie's Close to tell Torrence and Waldie that he was missing.

'Some beggar-woman must have stolen him,' Helen Torrence surmised, while Jean Waldie urged her to have it 'put to the Clap', and cry his disappearance through the town. But their response was a little too casual, and naïve Janet's suspicions were at last aroused.

She went purposefully to Mrs Auld's stable at the top of Horse Wynd where John Fair worked as an ostler. Had he given Helen Torrence eighteen pence to make his wife an apron and a handkerchief, she asked? John Fair laughed at her.

'I have too much use for my money!' he replied.

With this confirmation that she had been deceived, Janet hurried back home to raise Stonielaw's Close against her false friends. Her husband had already gone to work taking Charles with him, but the Close buzzed with the news that Helen Torrence and Jean Waldie had stolen little John Dallas.

At six in the evening the chairman had finished his work and Gilbert Gow's good wine was putting him in a mellow mood. His wife came timidly and asked him for the house key which he gave her. She still dared not tell him their son was missing, and he stumbled home drunk at midnight, unaware that his home was the centre of a tragedy.

His son's body, meanwhile, had been transferred that night from Anderson's lodgings to an empty room in Cowgate where the medical students intended to start their dissection the following evening.

John Dallas woke on Thursday morning to find his wife crying. She saved herself a beating by pretending to believe that she thought the child would have been with him; her husband only berated her on learning the boy had actually been missing for thirty-six hours, and the two parents set off separately to search for him. The goodwives of Stonielaw's Close advised Janet to go and tax Torrence and Waldie with the theft, but when she did so they denied all knowledge of it. Helen Torrence, however, was panicked into making a bad mistake. On learning that Stonielaw's Close blamed her, she went over there to establish an alibi.

Margaret Butter, the wife of an ironmonger, was at her door trying to learn what missing child was occasioning all the rumpus in the court when Helen arrived. Helen told her it was John Dallas, and added, 'They blame me.'

'What should make them blame you?' asked Mistress Butter.

'I canna tell,' replied Helen, 'but I am sure I was not out of my house all Tuesday.'

'I am sure I saw you at my house last Tuesday,' was Mrs Butter's crushing response. Helen had foolishly forgotten speaking to the ironmonger's wife when she cased the joint.

That night Flint, Arthur and Anderson opened John Dallas's lower abdomen, and examined the muscles to the left of the belly. The following night they exposed the muscles on the opposite side, and were about to make further incisions when word reached them that their subject was cried missing and foul play was suspected. Quickly the students sewed the body up again, and dumped it in a close off Libberton's Wynd where it was found the next day. It had obviously been in surgical hands, and the authorities sent for John Dallas who identified his son.

When the authorities heard the neighbours' stories, they arrested the whole boiling. John Dallas, Janet Johnston, James Flint, James Arthur, Andrew Anderson, Helen Torrence and Jean Waldie all found themselves in custody and subjected to separate interrogations before the magistrates.

Torrence and Waldie immediately pioneered a practice that would be followed by all their successors in murder for the anatomy market. They made self-exculpatory statements blaming each other.

The students and parents were released and the two women were thrown into Edinburgh's ancient prison, the Tolbooth, to await the sitting of the Court of Justiciars.

The winter turned hard, with the heaviest snows in living memory. Villages in Scotland were cut off. Benighted travellers froze to death. The Tolbooth gaolers were so occupied with keeping themselves warm that they let some gypsies break the bars of their windows and get away. But Helen Torrence and Jean Waldie were chained by the leg to an iron bar at ankle height.

Eighteenth-century Scotland gave a higher priority than England to the rights of panels (as Scottish defendants are called). A slow and careful examination of evidence to determine the libel (indictment in the Scottish courts) concluded with a laborious statement that the accused had taken John Dallas alive from his parents' house without their knowledge or permission, and soon afterwards sold his dead body to surgeons. On 3 February when this was read out and a jury empanelled, Mr Thomas Miller, who appeared for Torrence and Waldie, argued strongly that this was no capital charge, as the libel did not claim that the panels had harmed, let alone killed the boy, and it was very doubtful whether selling a body to the surgeons was an offence at all in law.

Five red-robed judges tried the case: Lord Tinwald, the Lord Justice Clerk, presided over the bench and enjoyed the support of Lords Minto, Strichan, Elchies and Drummore. This impressive weight of legal learning turned to hear the argument of Advocate Deputy, Alexander Home, for the Crown. Mr Home agreed that taken as two separate charges, neither of the acts libelled might be punishable. But he submitted that taken together they led to the inevitable inference that a capital crime had taken place. The fact that the defendants had promised the students a body, kidnapped a living boy and swiftly sold his dead body, led to an obvious conclusion which the process of law should test. The judges agreed that there was a charge to answer, but assured the defendants that they would have every opportunity to bring out all the exculpatory and alleviating facts and circumstances.

Unhappily for the panels, the only evidence as to how John Dallas had died lay in Helen Waldie's sworn statement before the magistrates. She said that when she found the boy looking over the window-sill:

> . . . she took him in her arms and brought him directly to her own house, and was Immediately followed by the said Helen Torrence; that before she came in, she [the deponent] gave the Child a Drink of Ale, but that it would scarce go over, and that it died in about six Minutes.

This allegation of sudden natural death would require some support from the evidence of those who had seen John's state of health earlier that day. They all contested it, John Dallas the chairman going so far as to say that his son was healthier on the day he died than he had been at any time since he was taken on the family outing to shear the harvest on their patch of land in the country the previous autumn.

When the evidence had all been heard, and concluding arguments put by the prosecuting and defending advocates, the jury deliberated from 5.00 to 6.00 p.m. before the judges adjourned for the night and allowed them the next day to make up their minds.

At 1.00 p.m. the following day, the jury returned and gave their verdict that:

> ... the Pannels are both guilty Art and Part of stealing
> John Dallas a living Child, and Son of John Dallas
> Chairman in Edinburgh from his Father's House at the
> Time and in the Manner libelled, and of carrying him to the
> House of Jean Waldie one of the Pannels, and soon
> thereafter on the Evening of the Day libelled of selling and
> delivering his Body then dead to some Surgeons and
> Students of Physick.

Which was all correct, legal and formal, and left it to the judges to decide whether the libel, now proven, entailed hanging the women. The judges gravely deferred handing down sentence until the following day.

When they reassembled to do so, Helen Torrence forestalled them by pleading her belly. The court appointed Mrs Knox, an Edinburgh midwife, with a team of four other experienced women to examine Torrence and report back whether she were really pregnant on the following Monday 10 February.

Three of this Jury of Matrons appeared at 'Eleven in the Forenoon' on that day. They reported that Helen Torrence was not pregnant, and had so confessed to them while they examined her. Lord Tinwald thereupon sentenced Helen Torrence and Jean Waldie to be hanged in the Grassmarket on 18 March.

The month's delay allowed time for the women to repent, confess and absolve their accusers, judges and executioners. In Jean Waldie's case, this gratifying end was achieved. In her last speech from the scaffold she admitted that she had been very drunk when Helen Torrence persuaded her to fetch the child alive from Stonielaw's Close. She had carried John in her gown-tail, and found him dead on her arrival back at Fairlie's Close. She believed he had smothered in her clothes as she carried him, and confessed that her death was just, as the boy had perished in her hands. She 'died in a very penitent manner, and gave the highest Satisfaction to all present,' according to the *Scottish Mercury*.

Helen Torrence, on the other hand, 'behaved with Decency, but seemed not to have an equal Sense of the Crime for which they suffered.' Indeed, she declined to say anything at all about it. But like her partner-in-crime, she admonished the spectators against drunkenness, bad company and uncleanness, which had brought the two to their salutory end. And the pioneers of burking, eighty years before Burke, were almost entirely forgotten.

FOUR

The Ben Crouch Gang

Between 1800 and 1828 resurrectionism in London grew from the obscure activities of a handful of men, easily supplying a dozen or so anatomists' demands, into a considerable trade with national ramifications and a good deal of transportation of cadavers between England, Scotland and Ireland. This is the period that made bodysnatching famous. As late as 1791 there was no generally accepted name for the practice, and few people had heard of it.

Ten years later there was still one anatomist dissecting secretly behind locked doors at night as though he were the mad scientist of Gothic fiction. This 'Mr C–' came to light when his resurrectionist, Hendricks, was caught carrying the body of a young woman past St Sepulchre's Church. It transpired that 'Mr C–' had rented a disused pub in Wych Street (where the Aldwych now runs); changed all the locks; had the rooms refitted for dissection; and buried the remains of his subjects in the cellar. But 'Mr C–' (who is not easy to identify) was a relic of the past. Anatomical professors, lecturers and demonstrators had facilities at the hospitals: Cline and Cooper had dissecting rooms at home and work. Perhaps John Hunter's devoted assistant William Clift was inadequately supplied with experimental space by the College of Surgeons for his interest in osteology.

A vast increase in student numbers contributed to better professional conditions. At the same time, the old supply of cadavers became utterly inadequate. Five-fold expansion in the teaching of anatomy at the London hospitals brought 500 students trying to share the twelve or so bodies officially available annually in the capital. An equal number in Scotland demanded their share. Provincial hospitals also wanted a few bodies, and anatomists required fresh subjects for pure research purposes. There were further increases in student numbers in 1809 and 1825. All professors of anatomy agreed that each student ought to work on at least two bodies before being licensed to practice surgery. The most dedicated would have preferred at least three and possibly five! Since the students dissected in groups around each cadaver, the more modest estimate still required something like 300 bodies a year for London alone.

Increasing student numbers created enlarged anatomy schools and dissecting academies. St Thomas's, St Bartholomew's and the London Hospital all built substantial dissecting theatres, which were expanded during the period so that they could contain at first upwards of forty and ultimately around 200 students, all working at one time. The Great Windmill Street theatre under the direction of William Cruikshank, Sir Charles Bell, James Wilson and later Sir Benjamin Brodie catered to the needs of St George's and Westminster Hospitals' students.

But with Marshall gone, two new anatomists established private schools and took pupils in competition with the great hospitals.

Joshua Brookes was nearly forty when he opened his school at the turn of the century. He was a passionate comparative osteologist. His brother kept the menagerie at Exeter 'Change and supplied him with dead animals to dissect and articulate. Joshua spent all his money on buying additional animals, and by the time of his death in 1833 he had assembled the best collection of mammalian bones and skeletons in London.

He lived for his science; resided over his theatre, and rarely left the building, which was at the foot of Blenheim Steps, between Oxford Street and Great Marlborough Street.

Brookes found that by injecting subjects (human or animal) with nitrate he could delay the putrefaction of flesh in hot weather. His house smelt like a ham-shop in consequence, but he was able to take students during the long vacation when Windmill Street was closed.

According to J.F. South – no great friend to the private anatomists: 'He was deservedly and generally esteemed as one of the best – if not the best – teacher of practical anatomy in London.' He was a Fellow of the Royal Society and his unquestioned talents should have made him a Fellow of the College of Surgeons and a hospital professor. These honours never came his way because he was not a gentleman and he was too dirty.

> Joshua Brookes [wrote South] was without exception the dirtiest professional person I have ever met with; his good report always preceded him, and his filthy hands begrimed his nose with continual snuff. In his ordinary appearance I really know no dirty thing with which he could compare – all and every part of him was dirt.

Joseph Carpue, who opened a private anatomy school in Dean Street, Soho, in 1800, was definitely clean and a gentleman. A Roman Catholic of good family who had made the Grand Tour in 1782, he dabbled in bookselling, acting and law before training as a surgeon at St George's, and he was swiftly given a staff appointment at the Duke of York's Hospital, Chelsea and a consultancy at St Pancras. He was also a Fellow of the Royal Society. Early in his career he tried to repay anatomy's debt to graphic art. At the request of Benjamin West, the painter, he crucified the body of an executed murderer to show how it hung.

But again, the teaching hospitals refused to appoint him. They regarded him as unacceptably eccentric. His teaching methods entailed catechizing students on information they had received. The hospital lecturers, who preferred to expound without interruption, claimed that this was unpopular and led to his having very few pupils. In fact, his classes were crowded from 1800 to 1830 and Carpue prospered exceedingly, charging 20 guineas a course and lecturing thrice daily on anatomy and twice a week in the evenings on surgery. His lectures were best remembered for his pioneering use of the blackboard, which gained him the nickname of 'the chalk lecturer'.

The leading light among the hospital surgeons of the period was Sir Astley Cooper. The favourite pupil of Henry Cline at St Thomas's, he was appointed demonstrator in 1789, lecturer in 1791, became lecturer to the College of Surgeons in 1800, and consulting surgeon to Guy's in 1825. He built up an extremely lucrative practice, and was created a baronet in 1821 after attending the royal family.

Rich, elegantly dressed, handsome and not unduly intellectual, Sir Astley became President of the College of Surgeons and the national *beau ideal* of a successful sawbones. It is unsurprising that he was a little vain. His students were quietly amused at the pleasure he took in illustrating the structures of the leg by sitting on his desk and outlining the position of muscles and nerves on his own elegantly-turned, silk-stockinged calf.

It did this child of fortune no harm that he was recognized as a very successful employer of bodysnatchers: semi-criminal associates were a manly common touch gilding refinèd gold. The resurrectionists themselves would have been neither pleased nor surprised that their friend and patron privately described them as 'the lowest dregs of degradation'.

In the 1790s Cooper bought Henry Cline's house in St Mary Axe and established a private dissecting theatre in the basement. He came to an arrangement with the Tower of London menagerie and received dead animals from them. When the elephant died it was far too large to be brought into the house. Cooper laid it out in the courtyard, hung carpets over the street railings to deter onlookers from blocking the road, and dissected it out of doors. He was also determined to have its skeleton articulated, and to this end called on Daniel Butler, one of the superintendents of the dissecting rooms at St Thomas's Hospital.

Butler's father had been an articulator and dealer in teeth, and Daniel followed in his footsteps. The best dentures at the time were not artificial teeth, but mounted sets of human teeth extracted from corpses, and they were in themselves valuable merchandise. Since anatomists after Hunter had little use for teeth, Butler was well placed to acquire saleable commodities by working as the surgeons' caretaker.

In the winter of 1801 Butler did Cooper a further service. A dispute had arisen between the resurrectionists and the hospital porters, probably because the increased demand for bodies led the suppliers to ask higher prices. But the bodysnatcher named Bill Harnett, whose wheedling Irish deference made him a particular favourite of Cooper, was willing to supply subjects when his comrades were at loggerheads with the hospital. To avoid upsetting the porters, these bodies were left in hampers at Cooper's private gateway, where Butler would collect them and take them by coach to the Borough. One night Butler had three hampers in a cab when the driver stopped suddenly at the Coach and Gate Inn in Gracechurch Street and called out to the ostler that he didn't like the look of his load. Butler slipped swiftly out of the offside door and ran back to St Mary Axe. Forewarned, Cooper went straight to bed, and was tucked up in his nightcap when the watch appeared at his house to ask why three dead bodies had been collected from his gateway. The surgeon glared at them from his bedclothes, and declared he was not responsible for parcels dumped on his premises by unknown persons. The watchmen apologized for disturbing him, but said they would have to report the matter to the Lord Mayor. Cooper was up at dawn and hurried over to the Mansion House, where the Lord Mayor assured him he would hear no more of the matter.

Such connivance by magistrates was normal. They had no wish to be accused of hindering medicine or learning, and it led the surgeons to believe that they were essentially within the law. (Even 'Mr C–', the secret corpse-collector of Wych Street, was never called before the courts.) Butler was less secure, but his next significant action was to put him quite beyond legal protection.

In 1803 he was found concealing £200-worth of silk. His claim that he dealt in cheeses and ribbon at Wood Street completely failed to convince the Worship Street magistrates. They fined him £20 for possession of stolen property and confiscated the silk while they made enquiries for its true owner. Butler's character was lost. He left the hospital and joined forces with another occasional receiver of stolen cloth.

This was Ben Crouch, son of a Guy's Hospital carpenter. He and Butler at some time jointly received the loot from a warehouse robbery in Watling Street and boasted to the surgeons that they were wearing suits made from the haul. But fencing was not Crouch's main occupation. He was the leading resurrectionist in London, heading the most powerful gang of bodysnatchers ever seen before or since. From 1809 to 1813 he secured a virtual monopoly of supply to the United Borough Hospitals and St Bartholomew's.

Ben Crouch liked to be described as a pugilist. He was a tall, powerful man with a harsh voice and a pock-marked face. Like many of 'the fancy' he was a sharp dresser, favouring frilled shirts, gold rings and heavy seals. He encouraged an enthusiasm for boxing in his gang, some of whom claimed to be great fighters and capable of defending themselves against Crouch himself. On the days of big prize-fights the whole gang would abandon bodysnatching to go and see the bout.

Well known to the magistrates, Crouch was not an ideal spectator at the secret and illegal boxing matches. The press described him as a well-known or notorious pugilist. Non-sportsmen were frightened by his bullying aggression. His flash presence by daytime in a quiet suburban neighbourhood suggested that the prize-ring was being set up, and hostile magistrates might intervene and prohibit the fight.

Yet in the annals of boxing Crouch was very small beer. Pierce Egan never mentions him. The comprehensive listing in *Fistiana* of 1844 shows that he never fought for a prize under the auspices of the nationally recognized ring. Only H. D. Miles's masterly *Pugilistica* of 1880 proves that Crouch was truly one of the inner circle of boxing enthusiasts. In September 1816 he seconded a rather inferior black boxer named Sam Robinson in his match against black Baltimorean Henry Sutton at Doncaster Races. Robinson lost, with Crouch complaining vociferously that his man had been fouled in the opening round.

The London surgeons cordially disliked Crouch. They said he was impudent, bullying, artful and occasionally drunk. In his cups he was still more rude and aggressive.

He seems to have been decorous enough, however, at the

beginning of each academic session, when he would come to the hospitals and discreetly negotiate with the professors. Before cadavers were delivered, the price of bodies for the new season had to be agreed, and Crouch also required 'opening money' – a substantial advance (from ten to fifty guineas) for bribing the watchmen whose collusion was essential. The professors shrewdly suspected that most of the opening money stayed in Crouch's own pocket.

But their real objection to the man was his recognition that prices could be forced up in the resurrectionists' favour as long as they all stood together and refused to accept low payments. At the beginning of the Golden Age of body-snatching the average fee was two or three guineas for a full-sized body (one over three feet long), and a guinea or less for children's and tiny infants' bodies (known respectively as 'large smalls' and 'foetuses'). By 1812 this had risen to four guineas a body and by 1828 to eight or nine. On occasion, as much as fourteen had been paid.

The surgeons tried to defeat Crouch's demands by forming a cartel. This was known as the Anatomical Club, and every lecturer appointed to a teaching hospital was instantly elected to membership. It met and dined regularly at the Freemasons' Tavern, and its sole purpose was the regulation of prices and dealings with the bodysnatchers. When the trade ended the club disbanded.

But the hospitals' snobbish exclusiveness defeated their own ends. By refusing to admit Brookes and Carpue to the College of Surgeons and leaving them teaching privately they also left them outside the cartel. This gave Crouch the leverage he needed. The gang could survive for some time by providing the Blenheim Steps and Dean Street schools, while the hospitals had to make do without subjects until they agreed to accept the new scale of charges. Individual lecturers who still refused to come into line could be refused any bodies at all, so that Sir Astley Cooper was aware of some who had been forced to cancel courses. Helpfully, from Crouch's point of view, the students were keenest at the beginning of each session, just when the season's prices were being negotiated. They put pressure on the professors to see that bodies were available, and the anatomy teachers were aware that if dissection classes started late in the term, other interests would have supervened and the students would not bother to attend them. Since students paid lecture fees directly to the lecturer, the anatomists were financially injured if class numbers fell.

Naturally, Crouch had to make sure that the surgeons could not counter by finding an alternative source of supply. To this end, he set out to absorb useful individual bodysnatchers into his own gang and drive others out of business. He used four principal means to secure his monopoly. Simple violence was the easiest. He and his gang of boxers beat up any stray rivals they encountered. Shopping them to the law was the next tactic. Since the Crouch gang had constables and graveyard watchmen in its pay all over London, it was easy to arrange that any independents trying to break into the trade should be handed over to the magistrates before their careers had progressed very far. But if newcomers were too tough to be intimidated and succeeded in corrupting their own graveyard keeper somewhere, then the most scandalous of the four sanctions came into play. The graveyard would be 'spoiled'. The Crouch gang would dig up graves, and leave them exposed; throw putrefied and unmarketable corpses and bones on to the ground; litter the place with shrouds; and even hoist empty coffins up on the spikes on the walls to ensure that passers-by noticed. A spoiled graveyard was ruined from the bodysnatching point of view. Outraged local residents and relatives of the dead would institute immediate enquiries. Corrupt watchmen would be exposed and sacked. Vigilantes with guns would keep a close and effective watch over the place. But it had the disadvantage of making grave-robbing familiar to the general public. Bodysnatchers were cordially detested and risked serious injury by mobs if they were taken.

The final sanction was directed against the surgeons themselves and seems to have been pioneered individually by Crouch. If an anatomist succeeded in finding an alternative means of supply, then Crouch and a friend would break into the hospital, terrorize any doctors or porters on the premises, and 'cut' the available cadavers, shredding them into unusable remnants. It was risky, because the burglarious entry was felonious. But nobody ever questioned Crouch's courage.

By these means Crouch made himself 'King of the Resurrectionists' and achieved his approved monopoly of delivery to the hospitals by 1809. The only surviving rival gang was Israel Chapman's Jewish mob, based on Field Lane off Saffron Hill.

The Jews were a prominent boxing community (Daniel Mendoza had invented 'scientific' pugilism) and could not be intimidated. And Chapman's men specialized in stealing bodies from infirmaries and undertakers before they were buried, so the Jews were immune to spoiled graveyards. But Chapman was far too fly to diminish his own profits by trying to undercut Crouch, and he and Crouch ultimately divided the main market between them. The surgeons of the London Hospital were notorious for raiding their own mortuary to supply their needs without recourse to professional resurrectionists, until their chaplain protested that he would read the burial service over no more coffins full of bark and shavings. In the seasons of 1811 and 1812 for which figures exist, the London Hospital bought a mere 9 cadavers from the Crouch gang. By contrast, St Bartholomew's bought 124 over the same period, and St Thomas's 78, with 6 to the associated Guy's, and an additional 14 delivered as United Borough bodies. The Borough professors personally bought a further 29 corpses for private research.

Chapman must have supplied Great Windmill Street, which taught St George's and Westminster students and took only 35 bodies from Crouch over the same period, all bought in privately by the professors. In the major gang war of 1816 Chapman actively sided with Ben to drive blacklegs out of the business.

Still, Crouch was unable to force prices up by more than a guinea a body. The drawback was Astley Cooper's favourite, Bill Harnett, who took the view that it was commercially wiser to stay on the right side of the surgeons than to antagonize them by demanding ever more money. As long as he was a powerful force in the gang (until age began to take its toll around 1813) prices rarely rose above four guineas.

According to memoirs left by J.F. South and Astley Cooper's nephew Bransby, deferential good-natured Bill

Harnett hated Crouch and refused to work with him as a rule. But neither of them met the bodysnatchers until after 1813, and there is evidence that Bill was an acknowledged member of the gang (despite occasional rows) throughout 1811, starting to slide away during 1812. South also understood that wiry little Harnett was a fine boxer who could not be intimidated, and frequently thrashed Crouch. But Bransby Cooper reported that the two only fought one notable battle (at Wimbledon) which Harnett was winning until repeated blows to the jaw reopened an old injury and defeated him. South remarked that Harnett's looks had been spoiled by the loss of three teeth in boxing, and both surgeons seem to have relied incautiously on the Irishman's favourable self-description.

Experience was probably Harnett's strongest suit. He was the oldest of the gang and was probably bodysnatching as early as 'Lousy Jack'.

Crouch had a strong ally in Daniel Butler who followed him like a dog, according to South. The surgeons rather liked the little fat articulator. He had a smiling Sancho Panza-like good-nature. His weakness was gin, and when drunk he could become quarrelsome. But a soft answer usually served to dispel his wrath, and had he not been loyal to Crouch he might have become even more of a favourite than Bill Harnett.

He introduced Crouch to toothing as a separate activity, and after the Peninsular War began in 1808 the two made many trips to the Continent to collect teeth from corpses on battlefields. The bodysnatchers had themselves officially recognized as sutlers so that their camp-following was approved. And they made very substantial profits from this toothing, in addition to more ordinary looting of the corpses.

Bransby Cooper first met Butler on this caper. It was at Sarre in 1814 after Wellington's advance into France, and young Cooper was serving as an army surgeon. The little stout man, pitifully undernourished and sick, presented himself at Cooper's tent with a letter of introduction from his uncle Astley. He had lost contact with his companions and urgently needed food, medicine and assistance. Cooper saw him back to good health, and then despatched him to

England, firmly refusing to take an abhorrent battlefield looter under his wing for the remainder of the campaign. Butler wrote him a cheerful letter of thanks including the information that he had realized £300 from his expedition to the Continent.

The hospitals recognized Crouch and Butler as joint leaders of the gang, though they knew that Crouch was definitely the top man, kept records of the bodies supplied and prices paid for them, and controlled the distribution of money among the bodysnatchers. Indeed, it was notorious that Crouch arranged the pay-outs at public houses where he carefully remained sober so that he could cheat his comrades. This caused occasional friction, but Crouch's astuteness, strength of personality and willingness to deal firmly with surgeons and porters made him an indispensable leader, and his followers usually came back to heel after a brief mutiny.

Crouch's closest friend was Bill Harnett's nephew Jack. He was tall, red-haired and freckled, and like Crouch a notably flashy dresser. The surgeons found him even nastier than Crouch. He was 'the most disagreeable of the party . . . and very rarely had anything pleasant to say,' according to South. Bransby Cooper described him as ill-looking and uncouth in address and manner. He, too, joined Crouch on the continental toothing expeditions where, in addition to corpse-robbing under the cover of sutling, they burgled and looted abandoned houses. Jack Harnett was so ill-disposed that Bransby Cooper feared he and Crouch might well have murdered the wounded lying in battlefields in order to ransack their teeth and possessions.

The last member of the original gang was the least steadfast. All things to all men, Josh Naples persuaded the surgeons that he disapproved of Crouch and preferred working with Bill Harnett. He was certainly scabbing in 1813. But even the anatomists recognized that he was unreliable and never openly stood up to the domineering pugilist. And Naples was uncompromisingly on Crouch's side in the 1816 gang war.

He did not become a professional resurrectionist until 1804. As a young seaman he had served on HMS *Excellent* and fought under Nelson and Jervis at the Battle of St Vincent in 1797. On the ship's roster his Christian name was given as

Joshua : the press usually called him Joseph or Jos, and occasionally John or Jas.

Returning to land, he tried various occupations and eventually became a grave-digger at St James's Church, Clerkenwell in 1800. Here he was quickly corrupted by a Scotsman called White who was organizing the distribution of bodies to the hospitals. Naples developed the habit of opening the coffin before he filled the grave after a funeral, putting the body in a sack, and then gradually raising it higher and higher up the ground resting on the mould he shovelled in. He left it buried under a very thin covering of loose mould, so that it was easy for him to return and collect it at night.

By 1802 Naples was doing some direct dealing on his own account. St Bartholomew's students left hampers out for him, and he would pick these up for the delivery of bodies that he did not pass through White's agency. He sometimes took teeth alone, and earned a guinea a set for them. He was also given to cutting off heads, arms and legs which could be sold separately for demonstration purposes. But he showed himself a novice when he sent a message to undertaker George Atkins offering him some shrouds, caps, pillows and coffin-furnishings, saying 'they were very little worse for wear'. This, of course, was felony, and he would have been transported if charged with it.

Fortunately for him he was not taken until White was stopped and a body he had been carrying was traced back to the Clerkenwell churchyard. Naples was given two years in the house of correction, but managed to escape before his sentence was complete. Crouch promptly shopped him with an anonymous letter when he tried to maintain himself by independent bodysnatching, and on his final release he had little option but to join the gang.

For the historian he was to prove the most important of all resurrectionists. For he kept a 'log-book' of his nights' work, his companions in digging and selling, the churchyards they visited, and the surgeons who bought the bodies. And the sections covering late November 1811 to April 1812 and August to early December 1812 came into the hands of the Cooper family, passed to the College of Surgeons, and were published in 1896 with an introduction by James Blake Bailey. It is the most revealing account extant of the bodysnatching trade as it operated. It shows the gang at an important turning point as two new members were joining, whose influence would break the cosy solidarity that had ensured their price-fixing monopoly at the hospitals. And it has never been properly interpreted because Naples made a slip of the pen which combined with South's faulty memory to conceal most of Butler's activities.

On 30 December 1812 Naples recorded, 'Butler and Danl. took 1 large to Framton, large small to Hornig.' (Frampton and Hornig were surgeons.) This is the diary's first reference to Butler, who makes suspiciously few appearances. Since South had claimed that Butler's Christian name was Bill, and a couple of pages later called him Tom, nobody has ever associated him with the very active Daniel of the diary – a completely unknown figure, unmentioned by the surgeons or press reports of resurrectionists' arrests. But the discovery of Butler's conviction for receiving shows that he was, in fact, the mysterious Daniel ; and at once the composition of the gang falls into place.

Ben, variously called Ben, Benjn. and Crouch, is prominent: digging, selling, arranging share-outs, rowing, drinking, 'looking out' (following funerals during the daytime) and, once, cutting. Butler, almost as active, is consistently called Danl. until 30 December, and thereafter variously Butler and Danl. Bill Harnett is consistently Bill. Jack Harnett is usually Jack, and once, when he was nearly buried in a subsiding grave, J. Harnett. These are the original gang members.

Two new ones are introduced: Bill Hollis and Tom Light. Both are familiar from Bransby Cooper's account, where Light, still alive in 1841, is called 'L–'. Cooper was consistently protective of the few surviving bodysnatchers calling Naples 'N–', and a third informant who joined the gang later, 'Patrick'.

Hollis, according to Cooper, was a consummate villain. He started as a corrupt sexton, conniving at bodysnatching. But he became so extortionate that the gang exposed him, and he was forced to join them as an ordinary member. He was not

44

much liked by the others, so Cooper was told.

Light was a footman who served seven years on the hulks at Portsmouth after being caught stealing carriage window-glasses. On his release he became a bodysnatcher, but he was so dishonest that the others ultimately refused to work with him. Forced to earn a legitimate living, he exploited his brilliant talent for horse-handling, becoming one of the finest ostlers on the main post routes to the north. But whenever his fellow-workers learned that he had been a bodysnatcher he incurred such odium that he was forced to move.

At last he threw in his lot with some provincial Methodists, and affected unctuous penitent piety until they were touched, and took up a collection to buy him a horse and carriage to set him up independently. With the means of self-support in his hands, Light bade them farewell and came back to London where he was still leading a happily profane and unchristian life as a cab-driver in the 1840s.

Now Light may well have been a thief and Hollis a villain. But it is clear from Cooper's recollections and the evidence put before the Parliamentary Select Committee on the Teaching of Anatomy in 1828 that the bodysnatchers knew their patrons loathed larceny above all their other crimes, and they were quick to accuse each other of being thieves when they wanted to discredit rivals. 'Thieving,' said the retired Ben Crouch, when asked what other occupations his former associates practised: '*thieving*, most unquestionably ; but [he added virtuously] I have never been with them when they committed any other offences than raising the bodies, of course; but I am sure it is so.'

Cooper's principal informants were Naples and the later recruit he designated 'Patrick'. Both worked in competition with Hollis, and Naples had good reason to know that Light had brought dissension to the gang. And so Hollis and Light appear under unfavourable colours in Cooper's account.

At the time when Naples compiled his log-book, Hollis was still a sexton. He is first mentioned on 15 March 1812, when Naples 'Paid Hollis £11 11 0 at the order of Miss Kay'. This is a large sum – the value of two bodies and three sets of teeth or extremities. And Miss Kay was clearly neither a bodysnatcher nor a surgeon. A woman paying money to these men can only have been a private burial-ground owner. (Two elderly ladies, for example, owned a small cemetery at Mount Pleasant.) And a cemetery owner would not pay a grave-robber for despoliation. Miss Kay must have been paying Hollis for a substantial piece of grave-digging. Goodness knows how Naples managed to interpose himself as a reliable go-between, but he may well have reverted temporarily to the honest work of interment for the advantage of inveigling Hollis into association with the gang.

Three more pieces of evidence show that Hollis had not been exposed in the period covered by the log-book. He is once described as 'Mr Hollis' – a designation never accorded to Naples's fellow bodysnatchers. His payments were differentiated from the gang's thus :

> 10th Aug
> went to St. Thos. got paid for 1 adult £4 4s 0d. went to
> Bartholm. got paid £4 4s 0d. row'd with Ben did not
> settle each man had £2 2 0 left with Hollis £2 2s 0d. for
> Expences, at home all night.

The formulation 'for Expences' is consistently used in the log-book to describe payments to watchmen and constables. Hollis, we infer, was not yet a gang member. ('At home all night' means that the moon was too bright to make it safe to go out grave-robbing.)

Finally, Hollis twice accompanied the gang when subjects were delivered, but made sure he was not associated with them by the hospital staff.

> 16 August (Sunday)
> At night went to Harp's got 1 adult male took to Wilson 1
> Small Do. took to Barthow : a Porter carried the large.
> Hollis did not go in.
> 17th
> got 1 adult M. Danl. carried to St. Thos.
> Hollis did not go in

Hollis, then, was not yet centrally involved with the gang as he would be in the shifting alliances that ultimately led to the great break-up of 1816–17.

South gave the following account of the gang's periods of instability.

> Their mode of conducting their business was usually together, as one joint-stock company, who were under the entire control and direction of the greatest and cleverest rogue of the party, who agreed with sextons and others, and *made the places right* at which the work was done, received the money when the work was delivered, and then divided the spoil among his partners. As this fellow generally took care to keep sober, whilst the others managed to get drunk at the public houses where their financial matters were arranged, he very commonly endeavoured to cheat them of their due share, and often succeeded, Sometimes they were not so drunk as to be content with the allotted share, and then a row rose – perhaps a fight ensued ; the one joint-stock company broke up into two or three, and each endeavoured to anticipate the other in robbing the grounds with which they were all acquainted.

Naples' journal shows this happening in some detail. The first clear sign of trouble is that night of 10 August 1812 when Hollis received two guineas expenses after a row with Ben at St Bartholomew's and the consequent failure to settle. The following night, Naples recorded :

> . . . had information Crouch had cut the subjects went to St. Thoms. had not cut them, Bartholm. they had, went to differt. parts of the Town for orders, settled our Expence & what we had Recd. each man's share £3.1s. 2½d. one adult St Thoms. 1 London Do unpaid Do Bartholn. unpaid ; at night went to Hoxton, 1 Large yellow Jaundice sold at Brooks.

Now on 10 August the sale of two bodies for four guineas each (one at St Thomas's and one at Bart's) had divided as two guineas to each man, plus two guineas expenses to Hollis. Evidently three bodysnatchers shared that payment, and Ben was not one.

The following day he took his revenge by cutting the body he had seen go in to Bart's. At the same time Naples and his cronies would have received four guineas, for the sale of one body to St Thomas's, and they could anticipate another three guineas apiece on the half-bodies sold to Bart's and the London Hospital : a total of ten guineas which, divided between three, would have given them £3.10s.0d. each. Since each actually received 8d. or 9½d. less, they had 'expences' of £2.6s.4½d. to pay out, which sounds like a watchman or constable's cut of two guineas plus some rounds of drinks. In any case, Naples was working as one of a party of three at this time, whereas heretofore he had worked with the gang of five (himself, two Harnetts, Crouch and Butler).

For the next few days Naples worked with Bill Harnett, Light and, occasionally, Butler, assisted by Hollis. 'Crouch' (no longer 'Ben') was no longer a friend.

On Sunday 23 August intermediaries tried to arrange a reconciliation.

> Hollis met with Ben at St George's agreed to meet
> Lambert's with the seperate partys: met, lookd. at each
> other nothing transpired concerning the Business, our
> party went to Harp's could not get in private door being
> shut, came home.

'Lambert', who provided the neutral territory for this abortive peace conference, was no less than a Holborn parish constable !

'Harp's', where the gate was closed against Naples and his party, was another instrument of Crouch's enmity. For Harper, often abbreviated to Harp, was the burial-ground watchman friendliest to the bodysnatchers in these years. In 1811–12 they raised cadavers from his territory on sixteen occasions – more than any other source. This entry shows, however, that it was only by pre-arrangement with Harper that access could be gained. And a place that Ben Crouch had *made right* for his gang could equally be 'made wrong' for mutineers.

The next day saw a compromise brought about because both factions feared the Chapman gang might start poaching their markets if they remained at loggerheads.

> Our party went to Bartholm. met with Ben and Daniel
> partly agreed me & Ben went in the Cart to different places

to look out coming back by Charing Cross met the Jews
Drag touted till Dark and lost scent came home did not go
out that night

'Touted', Bailey tells us, means that they followed the Jews to
see what they were up to. Another expedition the next day
proved that Chapman had indeed started supplying Crouch's
hospitals:

Understood the Jew had brought a Male to Bartholm. Met
by appointment at the above place, had a row, came home
after looking out

The external threat produced a temporary armed truce. But
Naples, Bill Harnett and Light continued to operate independently with Hollis's support, and Crouch now used the
sanction of informing. Light was the first victim. He broke
bail, and then was retaken and on 13 October appeared at
Hatton Garden magistrates court. *The Times* described:

Thomas Light, alias *John Jones* alias *Thomas Knight* . . .
lately indicted at the Middlesex Sessions for stealing dead
bodies for dissection but did not appear for trial
[wherefore] a Bench Warrant was issued against him from
this Office, was this day, with his accomplice, one of his
bail, Patrick Harnell, charged with having been last night
found in the act of stealing three dead bodies out of the
parish of St. Pancras or St. Giles.

The pair had been arrested by the Hampstead and Highgate
horse patrol, and were remanded until the St Giles parish
officers could be called as witnesses.
   Who is this unknown 'Patrick Harnell'? Evidently one of
the Harnetts. The press was liable to christen any Irish
criminal 'Patrick' if they didn't catch the name in court. But
which Harnett, Bill or Jack? Naples's diary clarifies the
situation, and additionally shows that Josh himself was
furtively in cahoots with Light and his accomplice.

Tues 13 Oct
Went to Bartolm. me Ben Jack & Butler could not find the
others, myself came to Boro sold 1 small that was on hand
for £1. Came home afterwards went to Tomlight

understood he had recd. the money got £5 from him, came home, at home all night.

The missing 'others' were definitely Bill Harnett and Tom Light – the only two gang members not present when the muster was called at Bart's. And the reason for their absence is clear: they were in court. But none of the gang knew this at the time, and Ben, Jack and Butler clearly did not know that Light had managed to collect an advance before his arrest. Naples took his cut, and, judging by the sum, probably another man's (Bill Harnett's or Hollis's).

Still, the unstable gang continued to work together until the following year. On 19 November, for example, Naples:

> Met with Hutton at Smithfield, Bill me & Ben went to St T's got 2 ad. Jack remained with Hutton, the party went to Bartholm. Ch. got 2 ad. the whole Abernethy. Gave one to Hutton for information.

Since Hutton was yet another Holborn parish constable it is evident that Crouch had the watch there in the palm of his hand, and it is both interesting and surprising to see that the man accepted a body in payment. Abernethy, who bought all four subjects that night, was lecturing in anatomy at St Thomas's at this time, according to Naples. His career was essentially followed at St Bartholomew's, however.

In 1813 Crouch evidently lost all patience with the independent mutineers, and Naples embarked on that phase of his career that was to make him the most frequently arrested of all the Crouch gang. When he was taken before Union Hall magistrates, Lambeth, in 1819, the bench remarked how often he had been before them on similar charges. Bransby Cooper tells us that these frequent arrests were mainly the result of information laid by Crouch. And the first of them, in September 1813, caused Naples a little cynical amusement as *The Times* observed:

> 10th Sept.
> Yesterday a man who said his name was *Joseph Naples*, on a charge of stealing a dead body out of St Pancras new Burying Ground. When the prisoner was put to the bar, he looked with the most daring assurance; the eye of every

individual was turned with indignation on him, but particularly when the unfortunate wife and daughter of the deceased, dressed in deep mourning, were introduced into the office.

Lambert the officer stated, that about five o'clock that morning he met the prisoner with a large bundle on his shoulder near the St Pancras new Burying-ground; witness asked him where he was taking it to, on which the prisoner gave him a card with the address on it of Mr. Thomson, cutler, Windmill Street, Haymarket. On examining the bundle, the witness found it to contain the dead body of a man, tied up as close as a trussed fowl, and only covered over with a piece of green baize. He took the prisoner into custody, and went to the Sexton, who, on examining the ground, found the grave open, and the body missing that was buried there the preceding evening . . . .

The prisoner, as he was being taken from the bar, with an air of assurance, asked the magistrate, Mr Capper, was it not a bailable offence? he was answered that it was, on which he made a bow and retired amidst the execrations of all present.

Well might Naples feel cocky and assured. An arrest by the corrupt Lambert was merely an occupational hazard of gang warfare. The use of a spurious delivery address adjacent to a hospital or medical school was common practice among resurrectionists. Soon he was cheerfully in Maidstone Gaol, laconically recording his views of turnkeys and prisoners.

In November, Light was taken up again. A Mr Mason, passing through Newington churchyard at 6.30 on the evening of the second, found two watchmen searching for men they had information would be robbing the ground that night.

'They are in the ground now,' said one. And a little later, 'They are not far off, here are their tools.'

Mason passed the watchmen, and soon encountered Light and another man approaching him. He stopped them, informing them that they were certainly men the watch was hunting for. The unknown resurrectionist ran away, but Light hit Mason who promptly knocked him down. Griffin

the watchman led him away, Light protesting that he had
followed the trade for some time and would not give it up
now. When he reached court he echoed his crony Naples,
asking whether bodysnatching was not a bailable offence.

In February 1814 Light was stopped once more, this time
in the unquestionable company of Bill Harnett. At 4.30 p.m.
on Tuesday 15 February, officers Read and Matthews saw
'three known resurrectionists' driving a cart up Holborn.
Known or not, the constables must have been acting on
information to stop and search them on a public thoroughfare
in broad daylight. There was a fierce fight, and the men were
arrested. The cart contained seven bodies in boxes and bags,
which the officers decided had come from Bunhill Row Burial
ground. The prisoners were Thomas Light, 'Wm Arnott' (i.e.
Bill Harnett) and – Spelling.

This war reached its climax in 1816. Naples had by then
allied himself with Crouch once more. Bill Harnett led the
opposition, probably abetted by Light, and possibly Butler
who had dallied with Naples and Light in 1813, and was
surprisingly absent from Crouch's last stand.

At the start of the academic session Crouch demanded that
the price of subjects be raised from four to six guineas. The
Anatomical Club refused to negotiate, and Crouch ordered a
complete cessation of supply to the hospitals. After three
months' famine, William Millard, the St Thomas's dissecting-
room superintendent, persuaded Bill Harnett to supply
corpses at the old price. *The Times* report described Crouch's
response ironically in terms of industrial relations.

> A curious case of combination, riot and assault came on to
> be investigated before the Magistrates at this office [Union
> Hall magistrates' court] on Wednesday, when Benj.
> Crouch, John Maples [sc. Josh Naples], Pat. [sc. Jack]
> Harnett, Pat. Murphy, Wm Hollis, and Israel Chapman,
> well-known resurrection-men, were charged by Mr.
> Williams and Mr. Sparrer, students belonging to St.
> Thomas's-hospital, with assault and riot. It appears that the
> spirit of combination which has of late been so prevalent
> amongst journeymen mechanics has of late communicated
> itself even to gentlemen of the honourable profession

known by the vulgar appellation of resurrection men or *body snatchers*. A majority of this worthy and enlightened band, which is by no means numerous, have lately been to the continent on a visit to the famed field of Waterloo, as is said, for the purpose of collecting and importing into this country a cargo of *teeth*. On their return lately, a general meeting was held, at which it was determined that in future no subject should be furnished either to lecturer or student at hospital or lecture-room, for less than six guineas, the price up to this time having been four. This resolution was communicated to the surgeons, who, considering the demand as an imposition, determined to resist it, and having found means to induce two of the fraternity to secede from the general body, they were engaged to furnish subjects to a certain extent. They succeeded, but the general body having received information of an intended visit to the tombs planned by the two traitors, they gave information to the officers at the town-hall, who, in consequence of the information they thus received, surprised the two offenders in the very act of opening a grave, and took them into custody. This did not satisfy their vengeance ; for having obtained information that some subjects had been taken to St. Thomas's Hospital, the six defendants went there, forced their way into the dissecting-room, where Mr. Williams and Mr. Sparrer were, and drawing their knives, began to flourish them. Mr. Williams and Mr. Sparrer, alarmed, attempted to effect a retreat, but were pursued and brought back, and obliged to continue in the room whilst the defendants cut the three bodies which were lying on the dissecting table into pieces. Whilst they were thus employed, information having by some means been sent to Glennon, he, with another officer, went and secured all the defendants, and took them before the Magistrate. They made no defence, but said they had been very ill-treated by the surgeons, who could not do without them. They were all ordered to find bail to answer the complaint at the sessions.

Greatly as *The Times* enjoyed twitting organized labour with its new recruits, and much as it looked forward to the prosecution of the bodysnatchers, the senior surgeons were alarmed. They hoped that an exemplary sessions trial followed by stiff sentences for assault and riot would bring the resurrectionists to heel. While this was not the first and might not be the last case of 'cutting', it was by far the most extreme, and the mass invasion and terrorization of students was clearly intolerable.

But they had reckoned without Crouch's determination and his capacity to stiffen even such broken reeds as Naples. The gang made it clear that whatever the law might be, they were going to put their case as they saw it. *They* were the ones working laboriously under cover of darkness on cold nights. *They* received a few guineas per body while the professors received twenty guineas per student per course and untold guineas in operating fees from wealthy patients. *They* had lifted the risk of imprisonment from the shoulders of students and junior surgeons, who would have to go back to their own sacking-up if professional resurrectionists disappeared. *They* were threatened with savage retribution from the mob if they were taken. *They* were sneered at for 'combining', while the surgeons had long maintained the Anatomical Club as a united front to resist their demands. The surgeons encouraged scabbing rather than pay the labourer his hire? So be it. The world should know all the details.

Better not, thought Astley Cooper. Enough of the unpopularity of bodysnatchers already tainted anatomists' professional reputations. And his fellow-surgeons agreed. Negotiations were discreetly opened.

Stupidly, the surgeons thought their problems derived from one man and not an inequitable system. If they could get rid of Crouch – or perhaps Crouch and Butler – the rest would be leaderless, and free competition of labour, beloved of classical economists, should enable the surgical cartel to hold down the remuneration of the remaining resurrectionists. In return for the withdrawal of all charges, Crouch and Butler entered into recognizances and probably received some cash settlement to guarantee their retirement as well. In the words of a pamphleteer of 1825 who hated Crouch and the surgeons alike, Crouch:

retired with an easy competence, the fruits of his enterprise and industry and has since directed his talents to a less hazardous and equally lucrative occupation, that of a *dealer in human teeth*.

Butler seems to have left London fairly promptly and gone to Liverpool where he took up toothing and dentistry. His extravagance and weakness for gin, however, ate up his profits, and he was arrested when he tried to pass a banknote that had been stolen from the Edinburgh Mail. Tried and convicted for this offence, he was sentenced to death in Edinburgh, but spent some time in prison awaiting execution. Here his cheerful personality made him a favourite with the governor, and when he complained of boredom he was given a horse's skeleton to articulate. This unusual occupation attracted the attention of England's anti-Napoleonic allies, Archdukes John and Ludwig of Austria, when they were touring Scotland, and they laid his case sympathetically before the Prince Regent. The upshot was a pardon for Butler, which Bransby Cooper believed was conditional on his leaving the country. As far as St Thomas's was concerned he was never heard of again.

But Daniel was still living near the hospital in 1825, and had secured the lucrative monopoly of importing children's bodies from Dublin, which he sold to a new private dissecting academy in the Borough.

Crouch's retirement was more complete if less precipitate. He withdrew from the London bodysnatching scene gradually over 1817 and turned at first to the fancy's other love: horseflesh. He went to work for Mr Newman of Barnet, a postmaster who managed the mail-coaches from the Green Man. Crouch arranged the private hire of his horses, which got him into trouble in St Albans where he was said to be the terror of the neighbourhood. A rival Barnet postmaster, Mr Bryant, succeeded in obtaining Sir Robert Peel's patronage for the hire of four horses. Crouch, who had tried to intimidate the rival firm into relinquishing the desirable customer, now put his threats into punitive execution, whipping one of Bryant's servants until he ran for his life, and knocking out another.

He was charged at St Albans sessions for these assaults. His sullen defence was that the contest was merely the 'Piccadilly principle' of procuring passengers, and that while zeal might have led to improper violence on both sides, it was extremely unmanly of his opponents to have recourse to the law. The court was not impressed. Crouch was fined £30 and gaoled for two months.

In one way and another he had now, as Sir Robert Christison remarked, made the south too hot to hold him, and soon he was happy to accept a commission to go bodysnatching in Scotland for a season.

On his return he took lodgings near the Kent Road and went back to toothing. He had saved his money carefully, and like other prosperous resurrectionists he believed in real estate as an investment. He bought a hotel in Margate, but unfortunately it failed when it became known that the proprietor was a former bodysnatcher. He made a few more trips to the Continent in search of teeth, but this trade was becoming dominated by the Jews and Crouch found himself hard up. In desperation, some time after 1828, he embezzled money from Jack Harnett and fled to Scotland. Harnett, one of the most successful of the grave-robbers (he left £6,000 when he died), pursued him and prosecuted him. Crouch went to prison again for twelve months.

He was a broken man on his release. He lived in great poverty, and died suddenly while sitting upright in a tap-room near Tower Hill.

So ended the greatest of the resurrectionists, around the time the trade he instituted had itself ended. His achievement was considerable. He found bodysnatching the occasional and slack occupation of corrupt grave-diggers and hospital servants. He established a small, disciplined and hard-working body of men. Of the 194 nights covered by Naples's diary, 124 were devoted to the demanding labour of digging up and distributing bodies; 10 were entirely given over to settling-up; and moonlight made resurrectionism impossible on 47. Of the remaining fortnight, two nights were given over to boxing matches; one to the theatre; two to following the Jews and one to settling a dispute in the gang. There was only a total of a week in which the gang were too drunk to work.

This compares favourably with other early nineteenth-century artisans, and is not at all what the surgeons' accounts of the dissolute and desperate bodysnatchers might have led one to predict.

Crouch kept records of the business and was able to refer to them nine years after he had left it. One Scottish surgeon was not too proud to work alongside him, and he could pass as a gentleman when necessary. He stood up to English patrons who despised him, and he showed his gang how to unite to earn a decent living. At least three of his comrades died prosperous, and he himself was ruined by commercial misfortune rather than extravagance or incompetence.

He was a bully and a blackguard. He whined and belly-ached whenever he was thwarted. But he was no more unscrupulous and dishonest than the great capitalists who would make fortunes from railways, manufacturing and commodities over the next eighty years; no more arrogant and overbearing than a great Tudor courtier; no more cruel and ruthless than a Plantagenet monarch. He came a long way from humble origins, and provided a highly reliable service to science, albeit the scientists disliked having to pay for it. His epitaph is well expressed in a disgusted speech in which Sir Astley burst out with resentment against him: 'an individual possessing considerable talents . . . impossible to compete with . . . a clever fellow.'

FIVE

The Great Inflation

With Crouch and Butler out of the way things grew worse for
the surgeons rather than better. Murphy, first mentioned as a
gang member in the great cutting assault of 1816, became the
new leader. He had barely possessed a shirt to his name when
Crouch recruited him. By 1825 he would be advertising for
house property to buy as an investment, and a hostile
pamphleteer cynically suggested that he was in the market for
a country estate next to Sir Astley Cooper's own rural retreat.

Murphy (his Christian name may or may not have been
Patrick, as *The Times* reported) had Irish charm and that
forelock-tugging deference which so appealed to the surgeons
in Bill Harnett, Daniel Butler and even Josh Naples. He had a
flat, open face, a sense of humour and civil manners. He was
rarely drunk, and was persistent rather than vehement in
making his point. Bransby Cooper described him as the most
intelligent uneducated man he had ever met, and seems to
have felt little resentment of the way in which that cleverness
was used to double the price of subjects in a few years.
Murphy used cunning where Crouch had used confrontation,
and it made him a more palatable associate.

The cunning was used on the gang as well as the hospitals.
Naples's diary proves that Crouch's settlings-up were rather
less dishonest than Cooper and South believed. But it is

entirely probable that he skimmed the 'opening money', which he negotiated alone. And Murphy went one further, inventing 'finishing-money': a bonus or retainer paid to the gang at the end of the season and related to the number of bodies they had fetched. Eventually Sir Astley had to pay over the bonuses in the presence of the experienced and suspicious Naples and a new recruit named Wild or Wildes, who seems to have become Murphy's closest associate.

Hollis, too, was a major bodysnatcher in the last phase of resurrectionism. A full member of the gang when they invaded St Thomas's dissecting-room, he shared with Crouch, Jack Harnett and Murphy the capacity to save his profits. These he invested wisely in a horse and cart. Throughout 1811 and 1812, transporting large numbers of bodies always required negotiation with carters. A 'dispute about the horse' at the 'Harty Choak' tavern at the end of December 1811 wasted a working night. Twenty-four pounds had to be paid out in settlement for it the following day – a very high outlay compared with bribing constables and watchmen. The horse and cart was needed again in August 1812, and Wortley, a Lambeth constable, collected the fee from the gang. Hollis won a commanding position once he owned the means of conveying seven or more bodies at one time. By November 1822 his prominence was acknowledged when two new independents named George Harris and Thomas Wallis were taken in the Borough.

They had made a good start towards monopolizing Crawford's Burial ground near Ewer Street. They bribed the grave-digger, John Hill, and learned the location of a newly-buried child. For five shillings and some beer he furnished them with the layout of the cemetery and promised a soap impression of the vault key, which would give them unrestricted access to gentlefolks' bodies. Yet as soon as their business seemed well established they were interrupted digging up the child's grave. They ran away and hid in a privy, but were hauled out and arrested. 'They knew how they got into a mess,' they told the Union Hall magistrates, 'for Bill Hollis and Murphy, who were at the head of the profession, knew their success, envied them their increasing business, and lay in wait and had a "down" upon them in all directions.'

Co-operation between Hollis and Murphy was not common, however. The gang effectively split in two when Crouch and Butler retired. Murphy retained Naples and possibly Jack Harnett for a short time; recruited Wildes; and employed a coach-driver named Michael or John Woods for transport. Hollis took on Ben Crouch's younger brother James; made a newcomer called Vaughan his closest associate; and was named as the companion of an otherwise unknown bodysnatcher called Charley Austin in 1822, when John Cousins of Lambeth conferred with them while trying to purloin his deceased mistress, Susan Crouch, from the watching layers-out in her rooms.

The rivalry between Hollis and Murphy was more evenly-matched than that between Ben Crouch and mutinous Bill Harnett. The 'Mount Pleasant affair' seems to have been the breaking point. Murphy discovered the burial-ground, bribed Whackett, the keeper, and repeatedly raided it secretly in the company of the man Bransby Cooper calls 'Patrick'. This was probably Wildes, who was arrested with Murphy and associated with him in Astley Cooper's account books as regularly as Hollis was with Vaughan.

Hollis and Vaughan learned about Mount Pleasant, and went to threaten Whackett with exposure unless he cut them in. Whackett responded by taking them to a pub full of labourers, and then shouting: 'Those fellows are body-snatchers and are come here for the purpose of bribing me to let them raise from my ground.' An infuriated mob chased Hollis and Vaughan, who had to run for their lives. They took their revenge by going straight to a magistrate and informing him that Whackett had emptied his own ground. The court officers and bystanders went to Mount Pleasant where grave after grave proved empty, and only the two constables present saved Whackett from being buried alive in a deep grave.

Murphy had a long memory and an unforgiving heart. He once had his own son imprisoned for stealing £5 from him, and felt no remorse when the son lost his reason in prison. Now he waited at least a year until the opportunity came to inform on Vaughan, who was wanted for another crime, and have him jailed.

Hollis, meanwhile, used his other follower, James Crouch, to attack the Murphy gang. In February 1820, Ben's brother, who was described by South as 'a little, saucy, silly fellow,' and by Bransby Cooper as a liar and not very much use, watched Murphy, Woods and Wildes lift two large sacks over the wall of St Dunstan's burial ground off Portsmouth Street at 2.00 a.m., and drive them to St Thomas's where they were taken to the dissecting room. He laid information against Murphy and his men a few days later, and they were furious to find themselves up before the beaks. They were as impenitent as the great Ben had always been, and shouted abuse at young Crouch. *He* was a bodysnatcher, and had been since childhood, they claimed. He had gone to the burial ground with the intention of robbing it himself, and was peeved to find he had been anticipated. (This was probable enough.) Less likely was their claim that he maliciously invented the information against them, and they had all been somewhere else at the time.

A year after Hollis and Murphy co-operated to crush Harris and Wallis, Murphy took his revenge on young Crouch. He was charged with stealing an immensely fat gardener's body from a church in Beckenham. He had taken Hollis's cart with two coal-heavers as helpers. When the grave was opened he went down on to the coffin and tied a rope around the body's neck for the hired help to heave it to the surface. This was normal practice, but this time the body was so heavy that the rope broke, the corpse fell on Crouch, and he was injured. Still, he took it to St Thomas's and sold it for the splendid price of twelve guineas.

The court at Maidstone was openly told that two other resurrectionists had laid the information against him. It made a pleasant change from the vague 'on information received', or 'a respectable man dressed like a butcher told me' by which constables usually covered their role in enforcing discipline in the resurrectionist gangs.

Such discipline was now clearly at sixes and sevens. Ben Crouch's tight ship had fallen apart and the surgeons ought to have been dictating commodity prices as merrily as a multinational company negotiating with an underdeveloped, single crop mini-state. So how on earth could young Crouch squeeze twelve guineas out of St Thomas's?

The fault was largely Sir Astley's. Betwen 1813 and 1816 three promising young surgeons came to St Thomas's. Edward Grainger, John Flintwood South and Astley's nephew, Bransby Cooper, were clearly heading for distinguished careers. Grainger, the eldest, was the first to join the professional staff. In 1816 he became Astley's dresser, and he reasonably anticipated that the next vacancy as demonstrator should fall his way. He was disappointed. Astley was determined to forward Bransby's career at the expense of any rivals, and Grainger found himself unjustifiably passed over.

He decided not to trust his future to a nepotic patron, and, noting the success of Brookes and Carpue, determined on opening a private academy south of the river for United Borough students during the summer vacation. He hired a large attic in a tailor's house in St Saviour's churchyard and advertised his first course in 1819. The results were so successful that within three years he bought a disused Roman Catholic chapel in Webb Street, Southwark, and converted it to a permanent Dissecting Academy.

This need not have affected the price of subjects seriously. In the Soho region, where Ikey Chapman's writ ran, the Windmill Street collegiate teachers cold-shouldered, but did not attack Carpue and Brookes. All of them bought freely from the Jews (in the period of Naples's journal Carpue only bought four subjects from the Crouch gang) and so even the efficient Crouch had not made a really major impact on prices. But now Cooper told his staff they must do everything in their power to ruin Grainger. If the upstart succeeded with his summer schools, the great man announced, he would soon be drawing students away from them during the academic session.

Cut-throat competition among the buyers favoured the sellers. Grainger let it be known that faced with any threat of the Borough hospitals trying to squeeze him out by buying up all available bodies, he would pay well over the market price. And once he was committed to six guineas and more, St Thomas's had to come into line. Crouch's heirs had learned the lesson of solidarity where prices were concerned. And the hospital surgeons, who blamed Crouch for rising prices, had brought their increased costs on themselves.

Grainger's academy flourished. Edward died in 1824, but his younger brother Richard took it over very successfully, and was finally accepted as a lecturer by St Thomas's in 1842. His pupils admired him so much that they gave him annual testimonial dinners throughout the 1820s. And he received further support when *The Lancet* was founded by the young radical doctor Thomas Wakley, who deeply resented having had to become a general practitioner because the hospital surgeons' high fees and nepotism debarred ordinary students from receiving the best training in surgery. With the deliberately mischievous support of William Cobbett, he mounted a steadfast assault on the collegiate surgeons' secrecy, the incompetence of some of Astley Cooper's appointees, and the authoritarian ambitions of the Royal College. Cobbett further encouraged him to attack prosecutions of resurrectionists whenever these were based on the hated Vagrancy Acts – the earliest 'sus' laws.

Increasing student numbers also helped the bodysnatchers. There was another big expansion in 1825–6. University College, London, opened in 1828 and King's a year later, adding yet another dissecting room. Crouch would certainly have divided and ruled this increasingly mixed market. Even his warring successors could not fail to increase their takings under the circumstances.

Murphy claimed to be 'King of the Resurrectionists' throughout the 1820s, and the Coopers cheerfully conceded this title to his vanity, though Sir Astley's account books show that he made more use of Hollis and Vaughan when he had a special undertaking in mind: a long trip to the provinces in the summer of 1820, for example, when a country doctor reported that an interesting case had terminated in death. Hollis and Vaughan received £6 5s. travelling expenses for sacking-up the subject.

Late in the decade Murphy watched the rival partnership break up. Vaughan, according to Bransby Cooper the drunken and imprudent son of a stonemason, went down to Yarmouth in 1827, and made the mistake of passing himself off to a young woman there as unmarried. When she found she had been deceived, she informed against him, and although Astley Cooper paid out £14 7s. 0d. to send down an assistant with bail, the profligate resurrectionist was gaoled for two years. Cooper made Vaughan an allowance of ten shillings a week for the first twenty-six weeks of his imprisonment and let his distressed wife have six shillings.

On his release, Vaughan took his wife to a village near Plymouth where, with two other bodysnatchers and one of their wives, he set up house and began transporting bodies from the local churchyard. But incorrigible lubricity undid him yet again. His advances offended a neighbour's maid, and she told her master that the Vaughan household seemed furtive and criminal. He assumed they were smugglers, and passed the information on to the authorities. Unluckily for Vaughan, a former Bow Street Runner named Ellis had just come down to organize the Plymouth police. He recognized the infamous London resurrectionists; watched the family, disguised in smock frocks, attend a funeral; and observed them robbing the grave at night. When their house was searched grave-clothes were discovered along with several bodies. Vaughan had made the fatal mistake of committing felony rather than misdemeanour, and he was transported, never to be heard of again.

Hollis, on the other hand, traded merrily in bodies until the passage of the Anatomy Act in 1832, and on 19 April that year enjoyed the distinction of being the last resurrectionist arrested before the termination of the trade.

Murphy did not confine his jealous control of rivals to outsiders. His close associate Wildes aroused his envy by perfecting the device of visiting workhouses and infirmaries with his wife, claiming to be next of kin to the recently deceased, and accepting the bodies to relieve the parish of burial expenses. Helped by a porter named Couchman, the Wildeses made a particular success of this ploy in St Giles's parish.

When they refused to reveal the source of their increased income to Murphy, he entertained Couchman, amiably plied him with drink, and learned the secret. Murphy then insinuated that the porter would be a made man if he betrayed the secret to the workhouse master. Couchman did so, and the Wildeses were taken up and charged. Murphy's plan to convict them as well as 'spoiling their ground' foundered, however, on Couchman's stupidity. In court he let himself be led into testifying that he had personally practised the deception, and exonerated the Wildeses.

But for those who were loyal to him, Murphy was probably a safer leader than Crouch. Naples's repeated arrests seem to have stopped after he was taken up in 1819 with one George Marden for stealing two children's bodies in Reigate. At any rate, Josh never appeared in *The Times* again, though he continued bodysnatching until the Anatomy Act, and appears in company with Murphy and Wildes in Astley Cooper's account books.

In September 1823 Woods was caught in Hornsey robbing a grave, which was being watched by two friends of the deceased. Two other resurrectionists escaped. But there is no other record of known subordinates of Murphy being taken.

Murphy might dislike his colleagues' working independently, but he had no hesitation in doing so himself. His most celebrated exploit was the discovery of a large locked vault outside a Nonconformist chapel. Murphy disguised himself in sober black garments, presented himself to the keeper, and asked if he might inspect the vault with a view to arranging his own and his family's future burial among the saints. In the course of his guided tour he contrived to slip back the bolt of a trapdoor in the roof. And returning at night he extracted every sectarian front tooth in the catacomb; an operation which realised £60 for him.

Murphy was also a key figure in the downfall of the only resurrectionist whose career caused Sir Astley Cooper a moment of embarrassment. William Millard was servant to Henry Cline. In 1809 he went to work for St Thomas's, and in 1814 became superintendent of its new anatomy theatre, built to hold 400 students for lectures, and 200 working in small groups around separate tables in its dissecting rooms. Like many of the surgeons' favourites, he proclaimed himself an expert boxer and persuaded his employers that he could beat off Crouch and Harnett when necessary. The great cutting break-in of 1816 occurred in his absence, and Millard claimed credit for having found the 'alternative source' of supply which provoked it.

He prospered in his work, taking every opportunity to make a little money on the side. He rented and sold overalls, dissecting tools and boxes to students, and spent his money freely, dressing almost as well as Crouch and eating and drinking heartily. If he genuinely fought his way through quarrels, he probably remained on reasonable personal terms with Ben; the freemasonry of fist-fighters prided themselves on taking loss or victory with sporting detachment.

But Murphy was not a pugilist. Millard was determined to protect his employers from his peculations, like taking advances and then selling the body a second time to another hospital; and when the bodysnatcher tried to make him accept a cadaver whose head had been crushed under a carriage-wheel as part of a job lot with a perfect subject, he refused. From that moment, Murphy was determined on revenge.

Two different accounts of his instrumentality have survived. According to Bransby Cooper, the bodysnatcher turned up at St Thomas's with a wheedling grin, and asked the surgeons whether they were not pleased with him for delivering five subjects over the previous two nights. The surgeons denied all knowledge of such deliveries, as did Millard. But a search of the dissecting rooms disclosed one of them, cunningly hidden under a wheelbarrow. Millard had been exporting them at a profit to Edinburgh: 'perhaps the greatest breach of confidence and want of grateful feeling he could have exhibited to his employers,' expostulated Bransby Cooper.

But according to Millard's widow, Murphy had merely to lay the (false) accusation that her husband had been moonlighting for Grainger to produce an explosion of rage from the jealous Sir Astley. Nor would the hospital administration help the dissecting-room superintendent, since he had sturdily refused to cast his parliamentary vote in accordance with the all-powerful treasurer's wishes. Even so, Mrs Millard maintained, her husband had not been dismissed, but cruelly made redundant by a staff reorganization of 1822, following his long illness in 1821. Surgeon Green had assured him that his thirteen years service had given entire satisfaction, and he should have any testimonial he needed.

Millard started his independent career by opening a chop-house in the Borough. He was popular with the students, and they gave him their patronage. But for quite blameless lack of business experience it failed, and he was now compelled to take up employment at Grainger's academy, doing very much what he had done for St Thomas's.

According to Bransby Cooper, on the other hand, the chop-house failed because the public would not take food from hands that had shaken bodysnatchers'. This forced him to become a full-time bodysnatcher himself, and he was arrested with Wildes when the pair broke into the London Hospital burial ground. The surgeons there had instituted a very close watch after Vaughan had rifled their mortuary. Enraged patients rose up from their beds to assassinate the resurrectionists, and they were only saved by the constables, who delivered them over to the magistrates for a three-month sentence in Cold Bath Fields Prison.

Mrs Millard's account differed again. Her husband had been collecting a body which the professors had legitimately arranged to leave for Grainger. When the watch took him, he identified himself as a former St Thomas's employee, but the United Borough surgeons refused to give him a character as he now worked for Grainger, and he was summarily imprisoned.

Both accounts agree that his employer bailed him, and Millard was sufficiently confident to bring an action for false arrest against the constables. This failed, and he was returned to prison, where he fell into a decline and died.

Mrs Millard felt she deserved some kind of pension or gratuity from the surgeons her husband hd served for so long. When they refused, she found a brilliant anti-anatomical journalist to write a pamphlet of protest on her behalf. *An Account of the Circumstances Attending the Imprisonment and Death of the late William Millard* revealed the whereabouts and activities of Crouch, Butler and Murphy in 1825 (the last actually living in St Thomas's Rents). It exposed Sir Astley's hatred of Grainger, and the collegiate surgeons' greed for student fees. It evinced detailed familiarity with St

Thomas's, and awareness of the London Hospital's scientific exploitation of the bodies of its own terminal patients. It treated Grainger sympathetically. It described the body price inflation as something of a scandal, and seized the opportunity to point out the deplorable poverty of Ireland.

All these features suggest close contact with the radical Wakley and *The Lancet*. But it cannot be by Wakley, as it also argues fiercely against dissection itself. It seems likely that Cobbett had a hand in its production; he may well have written it himself, as it is certainly the work of a hugely skilled propagandist. And Cobbett did not openly reveal his personal antipathy to dissection until 1832.

The pamphleteer puts forward one suggestion that would slumber until it was taken up in 1832 by the leading radical anti-anatomist. This is the proposal that all surgeons should will their bodies for dissection before they receive license to slip a knife into a cadaver. The pamphleteer also suggests that they should make sure that their friends' and relatives' bodies end up under the knife. He makes mischievous play with the boost it would give morale were Lady Cooper to die suddenly (which heaven forfend!), and Sir Astley assuaged his grief by exhibiting her vital organs to his students.

And he put one argument the surgeons really feared, as it was immensely prejudicial to the concept of dissection as necessarily detached and scientific. Says the pamphleteer:

> Who, we may ask, even among the practitioners of medicine, does not shudder at the mere contemplation that the remains of all which was dear to him, of a beloved parent, wife, sister or daughter, may be exposed to the rude gaze and perhaps to the INDECENT JESTS of unfeeling men
> . . . .
> We should observe that this is not mere surmise. It is impossible to be more explicit; we must therefore content ourselves with remarking with reference to such occurrences, that what has happened heretofore may, and in all probability will, happen again.

The Coopers hated this pamphlet, but wisely made no attempt to answer it. They allowed the scandal to die down and at last claimed that its exaggerations had rendered the whole production obnoxious to sensible people.

The increased cost of cadavers distressed the surgeons as they had to subsidize students who could not afford the full market price for the cadavers they worked upon. Yet they had no intention of reducing the amount of dissection imposed on students, for this would have reduced their own income from teaching fees. Rather, the Royal College (as *The Lancet* complained) was consistently at pains to increase the amount of practical dissection required of students, and tried to insist that the instruction be given by collegiate surgeons in the teaching hospitals.

John Southwood Smith published an article in the *Westminster Review*, reprinted as a pamphlet, *The Use of the Dead to the Living*, in which he expounded the importance of anatomy to medicine, and urged the introduction of the continental system whereby all unclaimed bodies from hospitals and workhouses were automatically handed over for dissection. As a radical, he argued that this would benefit the poor, since without cadavers, surgeons would be reduced to experimenting lethally on live patients in difficult cases. And he urged all good men and true to will their bodies for dissection. Jeremy Bentham, leading light of philosophical radicalism, did so, and also developed the eccentric notion of having one's head dried and one's carcase stuffed, so that an 'auto-icon' of one's remains might make a better monument than marble, or a true-life mummified puppet for stage representation of oneself!

The fee-price spiral attracted many free-lance body-snatchers to the trade: far more, indeed, than Hollis and Murphy could keep down by Crouch's well-tried methods of intimidation, informing and spoiling. All those in the know made frequent reference to 'the Spitalfields gang': impoverished weavers who had seen their hand-loomed silk priced out of the market by the Industrial Revolution, and turned to various forms of petty crime. Surgeons and 'regular' body-snatchers alike insisted that the Spitalfields men were very inferior resurrectionists. But the surgeons obviously bought from them, or the gang could not have survived.

None of their names were given in surgeons' memoirs, and the newspaper reports of resurrectionists' trials do not give their addresses. So it is impossible to identify the gang with certainty. But recurrent appearances before the magistrates certainly prove that throughout the 1820s a gang whose core may be identified as Davies, Shearman and Knapp was persistently active.

Davies seems to have been first in the business. Wortley, the Lambeth constable who arranged transport for the Crouch gang, acted on 'private information', when he took a pistol and a cutlass and arrested Davies with three men called Richard Tomlinson, John Thomas and Joseph Bedall on 17 December 1818. They were travelling up the Kent Road in a coach containing muddy clothes and digging tools, with the body of a tall man in the boot.

A large crowd followed them to the magistrate's office, completely showering them with 'mud and filth of every description'. And at Union Hall, two days later, they were charged with digging up Mr Pinberry from Plumstead churchyard.

Five years later, Thomas was taken again. This time he was in the company of John Shearing or Shearman and Thomas Kelly. Watchmen guarding the churchyard of St James's, Clerkenwell, heard them digging at 1.00 a.m. on 15 October 1823, chased them, and caught up with them as they scrambled out of the Fleet Ditch where they had tried to escape.

On 16 March 1826, Knapp made his first unsalubrious appearance in court. Two men giving their names as Thomas Coles and Thomas Watkins were loading a hamper containing the old and smelly body of an eighty-year-old man into his cab at White Horse Cellar, Piccadilly. Watkins told Sir Ralph Binnie and Mr Minshull, the Bow Street magistrates, that they had been taking the body to Sir Astley Cooper in the Borough. Sir Ralph pointed out coldly that he had seen Watkins a year before when he had been sentenced to six months for bodysnatching. Only then he had been using the name Williams.

That case had aroused no little interest at the Middlesex Sessions. A young man named King died of an undiagnosed congenital disease in Northolt. His parents realized that the surgeons would be interested in his morbid pathology, and had him buried ten foot deep with many large stones added to the soil. Nonetheless, on 29 March 1825 the grave was despoiled. The next day, villagers saw two men and a woman take a bundle out of a dunghill and carry it away on their cart. The three were arrested at Uxbridge, and the bundle, of course, contained young King.

The men gave their names as Thomas Mills and John Williams: the woman, who protested her innocence, was Margaret Lansdowne. Her husband testified that she had merely accepted the offer of a lift from two strangers. The court warned her against such imprudence and acquitted her, but sentenced the men to prison.

The abiding interest of the case is the name 'Williams'. There is good reason to believe that John Head, who used the name 'Williams' in 1831, had some bodysnatching experience before he teamed up with John Bishop in Bethnal Green. Head came from Highgate, a convenient district for a foray to Northolt. And this may well have been the earliest ascertainable appearance of one of the two London bodysnatchers whose excesses led to the termination of the trade.

Be that as it may, Watkins/Williams does not seem to have accompanied the Davies, Knapp and Shearman gang again. Shearman and Davies were taken on 1 March 1827, when a watchman named Rose, who had pocketed a bribe to let them rob graves in Clerkenwell, doubled his profits by informing Constable Sutton (?Hutton) instead. Two other resurrectionists, William Smith and William Pettit, were taken with them. Although Smith and Davies had chalked up arrests in the past, Shearman was the only one the court recognized as an old offender, and he was sentenced to three months in the house of correction.

He was at work again the following year, and taken with Davies and a man called Long, robbing a grave in Pentonville. Shearman amused the court immensely when his previous convictions for bodysnatching were mentioned. They didn't count, he insisted. The fact that he used to be a bodysnatcher didn't mean he was one now. The Duchess of St Albans used to be an actress, but she wasn't one now! This defence failed, and all three men went to prison once more.

Knapp was picked up again the following year carrying the

recently-interred body of a young groom called Matthews from Caversham to London. His previous arrest in Piccadilly was recalled, and he admitted that Shearman and a man called Bidgood had booked him to fetch Matthews for them. He didn't deny that he knew them to be bodysnatchers.

The recurrence of false and misreported names in the newspapers makes it impossible to identify any other cohesive gang. The recurrence of Shearman's unusual name and Knapp's occupation, however, makes this one decisive. And since surgeons and bodysnatchers alike referred only to the Spitalfields weavers as persistent, apart from Crouch's heirs and Chapman's Jews, it seems a reasonable guess that Shearman and Davies were indeed impoverished weavers.

Everyone asserted that the Spitalfields gang used body-snatching as a cover for theft. But the only resurrectionists individually recorded as being arrrested on such a charge were Hollis and a man called Cave, who were given six months at Maidstone for carrying housebreaking tools in their cart.

A name that was to be crucial in the annals of resurrec-tionism turned up in court in 1825. On 7 April that year, the Shoreditch watch heard that there were suspicious men in St Leonard's churchyard. They found John Jerron and James 'Blaze-Eye Jack' May lurking near a disinterred body, by which lay a spade and a pickaxe. Caught red-handed, it might seem. But prisoners could not give evidence and endure cross-examination at that time, and their counsel submitted the disingenuous defence that the two men might themselves have been trying to catch the real resurrection-men whose escape left them open to arrest on suspicion. All the lawyers in the court were hugely amused by the suggestion. But the jury was naïvely impressed and acquitted May and Jerron. May was, of course, a notorious free-lance bodysnatcher whose ultimate association with Bishop and Head would prove fatal to them and to their profession.

With bodysnatching hugely on the increase amid intense public awareness, defensive measures were naturally called into play. The first and most obvious was to set watchmen. These were easily corrupted and, indeed, the surgeons believed that they were without exception in the pay of the bodysnatchers. This was evidently true of Harper, Hill and

Whackett. The constables of Holborn and Lambeth (at least) were also effectively Crouch and Murphy employees. But John Seager, a sexton of Lambeth, proved incorruptible. Possibly this was because of his unhappy experience with turncoat watchmen in 1817.

Lambeth vestry was much exercised by the increase of grave-robbery that winter, and Seager hired extra watchmen to help him mount guard. William Marshall and Thomas Duffin were brought in, yet the graves were still despoiled. The cemetery was booby-trapped with spring-guns and man-traps, but the bodysnatchers were quite unimpeded. Seager then turned to his family and friends to help watch. At last, at 2.00 a.m. on 1 December, this vigilance was rewarded.

Seager, his son Joseph and Joseph's friend John Prince, all armed, were on the alert in the frosty night when they saw two men break into the grounds. The intruders went straight to the man-traps and sprung them. Then they walked leisurely over to the charnel house and fetched out two shovels, which they carried back to two new graves. By now the Seagers had recognized them. They were the assistant watchmen, Marshall and Duffin.

Seager let them start digging to incriminate themselves, and when he heard a blade strike a coffin lid, marched over, saying, 'You scoundrels! Don't you want some assistance there?'

Marshall swore furiously, and struck him with the shovel.

'Will!' cried Seager, 'don't you know me?'

'I know nobody,' replied the bodysnatcher, and swung at him again with the shovel. Seager parried the blow with his gun which went off, filling Marshall's right arm with shot. Marshall cursed, transferred the shovel to his left hand, and said, 'I'll do for you now!'

Young Joseph ran up, shouting, 'For God's sake don't strike, Will! It is your master!'

'I don't care who it is!' roared Marshall, raising the shovel in the air. 'I'll cut his bloody head off!'

Young Seager promptly fired a second shot into him, and father and son overcame their former employee.

Meanwhile, Prince, was in trouble. Duffin had stunned him with a sabre blow, which cut him to the skull. As he recovered his senses he realized that a second lethal blow was being aimed at him. In a frenzy he lashed out with the heavy poker he was carrying, struck home and felled his man. The fierce little battle was over.

Marshall and Duffin were committed for assault, and came up at Surrey Assizes in April. Their defence on the facts was feeble. Duffin claimed that they were only trying to see if the graves had been interfered with, while Marshall protested that Seager was always laying false accusations in order to curry favour with the vestry.

But Marshall's counsel put forward an interesting legal defence. He claimed that his client could not be accused of assault and battery with intent to kill, as alleged by the prosection, for he was legitimately resisting illegal arrest. Despoiling a grave was trespass, for which he could merely be ordered off the premises and subsequently prosecuted. Only felons could be forcibly arrested by private citizens, and Seager was a sexton, not a constable.

The jury was impressed by this argument, though common sense showed that the defendants had perpetrated unacceptable violence. It took some months before they were found guilty of common assault and imprisoned for two years.

Seager made another arrest in August 1824, handing over two men who gave their names as Jack Hall and Bill Smith. The latter was a persistent resurrectionist. He was taken the previous year bringing a cart with two bodies down Holborn Hill, and telling a most implausible story of having been employed by two strange men (who had disappeared when he was arrested) to hire the cart in Bermondsey, collect the bodies from Kensal Green, and follow the men to an unknown destination. On the other hand, the arresting constable, Batten (?Hutton), was equally implausible in claiming that he was walking aimlessly up the hill when a well-dressed man casually informed him that a cart was on its way down which would be worth looking into. Pretty clearly Murphy or Hollis was at work here, informing on outsiders. Three years later, Smith was taken again, bodysnatching in Clerkenwell with Shearman and Davies.

Since untainted constables, sextons and watchmen were rare, relatives and friends took to mounting their own watch over graves until such time as the bodies should be so putrescent as to be worthless for anatomical purposes. ('Thing bad,' was the laconic entry in Naples's diary whenever he dug up a useless rotting corpse.) Henry and John Powell guarding a friend's grave in Hornsey interrupted the Murphy gang in September 1823 and caught Woods. His two companions escaped.

Spring-guns and man-traps, as used by Seager, proliferated. The bodysnatchers sent their women-folk to simulate praying in cemeteries and putting flowers on the graves during the daytime, while actually noting the positions of the hazards. I know of no case of a bodysnatcher being caught by these devices. They were an ineffective and barbaric danger to the public.

Deep burial was very popular with those who felt responsible for bodies that might especially attract the anatomist. These were not only cases of unusual illness. Boxers believed that their perfect musculature was of scientific interest. Ned Turner, a Welsh lightweight from Bermondsey, was buried ten foot deep in Aldgate with heavy stones admixed in the soil. But the most famous boxer's burial, drawing a page of florid journalese from Pierce Egan, was that of Tom 'the Gas Man' Hickman.

'The Gas' should have been Champion of All England from 1816 until 1821, when Bill Neat defeated him and was awarded the title. Unfortunately, these were the last years when the great Tom Cribb basked snugly in his pub, his popularity and his claim to the title, without ever defending it against younger and fitter men. Soon after his retirement from the ring, Hickman, a notoriously bad driver, killed both himself and his passenger by overturning his gig in a terrible piece of drunken overtaking on the inside. He was only thirty-seven, and he was reputed to have the perfect physique. Egan relates the sequal thus:

> RUMOUR, with her thousand tongues, gave out that the surgeons required the body of HICKMAN, "to make experiments on," and his friends kept it eight days to disappoint them, whilst Bill Walter issued the chaff that "a whole peck of lime had been put into the coffin, right over

the chest;" a piece of gratuitous information that was given out with the very best intentions, no doubt. That the surgeons would feel a desire to have *the body*, or, indeed, *any extraordinary subjects*, there can be no doubt; but it is equally true that the anatomists of this metropolis do not go about to procure, *before hand*, the disinterment of any bodies, but their agents receive whatever may be brought to them. In consequence of such foolish notion, a grave of unusual depth (18 feet) was sunk in the church-yard, and the most scrupulous attention was paid to the *filling away*, Mr. Walter employing extra hands for that purpose, and placing a *watchman* near the ground several nights following.

Did Hickman rest in peace, eighteen feet below St Botolph's churchyard? Egan was wrong in imagining surgeons did not mark desirable corpses for sacking-up. Sir Astley Cooper boasted to members of Parliament that he could and did obtain any body he chose. The boxers were right in believing that perfect musculature ranked second only to deformity or disease in attracting anatomists' notice.

Hickman died in 1822. The year of Millard's contretemps with Murphy and dismissal from St Thomas's. And *Hickman's head was crushed by his own carriage wheel*. If Murphy risked the wrath of professional pugilists, bribed a special watchman, and dug eighteen feet through packed stony soil, all for a perfect specimen, he would indeed be outraged to have a mere lab technician reject it as old, mutilated and lime-burned. And Murphy outraged was Murphy vengeful. The sacking-up of Tom Hickman was probably one of the great, secret successes of resurrectionism. All to no purpose.

Perfect security from resurrectionists could be ensured by burial in Bridgman's Patent Iron Coffins. Edward Little Bridgman of Goswell Road invented them as an answer to bodysnatching in April 1818. Once sealed, they could not be reopened, and smashing them with sledge-hammers was out of the question for furtive criminals.

About a hundred were sold at £3.10s. each, and interred in fifty-two different graveyards, before a serious snag emerged.

London burial grounds were desperately overcrowded. Coffins were piled one on top of the other until many graveyards stood several feet higher than the surrounding ground, as may still be observed at, for example, St Peter's, Cornhill, St Helen's, Bishopsgate, or St Bartholomew's, Smithfield. Bridgman thought, under these circumstances, that his coffins, being smaller than conventional wood, were to be preferred. But where a graveyard was completely full and the coffins, shrouds and flesh in one section had turned to dust and clay, the sextons smashed their spades down through the remains, took the bones to the charnel-house, and started burying all over again. Since cast-iron rusted far more slowly than wood rotted, Bridgman's coffins were unacceptable to many vestries. Some refused them outright. Some demanded higher burial fees.

The Reverend Mr Clare, Rector of St Andrew's, Holborn, was put in a quandary when his parishioner, Mr Gilbert, turned up in February 1819 with the late Mrs Gilbert in a Bridgman's patent coffin. Mr Clare decided to permit the burial for this occasion only, and set a deliberately prohibitive fee. Mr Gilbert protested, and sued Mr Clare in the ecclesiastical courts to have the fee reduced. Before the case could come on, Mr Clare died, and Mr Gilbert was effectively non-suited with his wife still unburied. He appealed to the Bishop of London for permission to bury her, but his Lordship declined to intervene, on the grounds that the case was still technically before the courts. He suggested that Mrs Gilbert should be buried in wood for the time being, and then exhumed and reburied in iron if Mr Gilbert so wished. This, of course, was impossible. Bridgman's coffin could not be opened.

Five months later, Mr Gilbert was threatened with prosecution for keeping a body unburied. At this point, Bridgman came to his customer's aid. On 11 June he led a funeral party to the St Andrew's burial ground in Gray's Inn Lane, with the intention of burying Mrs Gilbert by main force. The sexton shut and locked the gates against her. A mob gathered, and accompanied Mr Bridgman and the coffin down to the church, where they demanded an interview with the minister acting as rector. He was not to be found. Mr Buzzard, the churchwarden, arrived, supported by beadles. The coffin was dumped on a tombstone while the beadles arrested Mr Bridgman for causing a disturbance. Mrs Gilbert was removed to the charnel-house to await the outcome of his trial. And, at this exciting juncture, *The Times* lost interest in the proceedings, so that this history is unable to relate what happened to her. Certainly she escaped the dissecting knife, as by now she would have fallen into Naples's category, 'Thing bad'.

The intense precautions taken by the bereaved of London during this last decade of resurrectionism stimulated a good deal of provincial bodysnatching. Mr Loftus, a coaching proprietor of Newcastle, suspected that his service was being used to ship corpses around the country. In 1826 he opened a suspicious hamper from Leeds weighing sixteen stone, and found the six-foot body of a hawk-nosed man. A gang in Liverpool, headed by John Henderson, was rounded up in the autumn of 1827. They had been shipping bodies to London and Edinburgh. Dr Gill, in the same city, had two houses he owned searched, after his gig was seen near a churchyard where a publican's daughter's grave had been opened. Her body, with the face stripped off, was found in one. A cadaver imported from Ireland and a child preserved in spirits were found in the other.

The London bodysnatchers moved out of town to work undetected. We have seen that Vaughan was arrested in Yarmouth and Plymouth. Murphy was taken in Yarmouth in 1825, and it cost a colleague of Sir Astley's £160 to secure his release. This is, perhaps, the most remarkable economic measure of the essential service competent resurrectionists performed for science.

In the same year, a London resurrectionist called John Johnson was arrested at the Star Inn in Portsea. He had taken a gang with him, corrupted the grave-digger at Colewort, where the Royal Hospital buried its terminal patients, and shipped a steady supply of cadavers to London. A constable asked him what was in his trunk at the inn, to which Johnson replied: 'For God's sake don't open it! There's a dead body, and I shall be torn to pieces by the people.'

Provincial judges were more severe than the London

courts. Johnson was fined £50 and jailed for six months. The grave-digger got twelve months.

A year earlier, Samuel Clarke of Haggerston, taken in Chelmsford for stealing bodies from Little Leigh cemetery, had confessed that the close watch kept in London was forcing the trade out into the country.

Students tried to help when the pressure became too great for the bodysnatchers. They received bodies at their lodgings to relieve the resurrectionists of the danger of transporting them through the streets. But cab-drivers soon learned that they could extort high fares from students taking hampers to hospitals. The Coopers heard of one who suddenly stopped at Bow Street magistrates' office, tapped on the window glass, and said to the student inside: 'Sir, my fare to So-and-so is a guinea, unless you wish to be put down here.'

With admirable sang-froid, the student replied, 'Quite right, my man. Drive on.'

To circumvent rising prices, London students and lecturers tried to emulate their Scottish counterparts, and involve themselves directly in obtaining bodies. John Flintwood South, as a young demonstrator, suggested to Murphy that he might make his own arrangements with sextons and watch-men instead of paying opening money. Murphy agreed amiably, and arranged meetings for him. The first took place in a dark and lonely court in Holborn. The watchman professed incomprehension at first, and then on hearing unmistakeably that he was being offered a bribe, exploded with honest indignation, and threated South with a pistol. A second appointment with a sexton in an even more out-of-the-way slum in St George's-in-the-East had exactly the same result. And South realized that Murphy had rehearsed his accomplices in an act, and had no intention of letting the doctors take away his livelihood.

Students could be excluded still more easily by extortion. Murphy introduced a group to some sextons who willingly agreed to let them dig up their own bodies, but charged such high prices for their silence that the young men found they were better off buying through the schools in the traditional way.

It was not, however, the great inflation that panicked the

surgeons into demanding legislative action to change the system. It was the determined provincial courts. The first straw in the wind was a Bedminster case of 1823. Five medical students from Bristol were charged with conspiracy to commit assault when they were found to be armed with bludgeons on a grave-robbing expedition. The highly emotional prosecution showed that some lawyers would attack the whole principle of educational dissection. Mr Palmer, for the crown:

> ... forcibly combated the alleged necessity of the act, by contending that although dead bodies might be necessary for the anatomical lecturer, in order that he might elucidate his theories for the benefit of his pupils, yet it was not only unnecessary, but even dangerous, to place subjects in the hands of unexperienced pupils, who, by making ignorant experiments on the dead, would erroneously fancy themselves proficients, and afterwards, by similar operations on the living, injure the health and probably destroy the lives of their patients.

The court clearly sympathized with this argument. The conspiracy charge was dropped on the ground that the students were basically respectable young men whose professional careers would be blighted if they were convicted of a felony. But older doctors and surgeons were uneasily aware that conspiracy existed as an offence of which they might be accused.

The axe fell in 1827. In Warrington, John Davis, a student, and William Blundell, a dispensary attendant, received the corpse of Jane Fairclough from bodysnatchers Edward Hall, Richard Box and Thomas Ashton. All five were charged with conspiring to procure and receive the body from the Baptist churchyard at Hill Cliff. Once again, the conspiracy element was dropped on grounds of clemency rather than law, so that it remained available for future use. And to the utter horror of the medical profession, the bodysnatchers were acquitted on a defence of mistaken identity, while Davis and Blundell were *convicted of receiving the body*. In May 1828, they were brought up for sentencing, and received fines of £20 and £5 respectively. For the first time since Lynn's case, anatomists were demonstrably in breach of the law.

The surgeons leaped into action the moment Davis's conviction was announced in March. Radical MP Henry Warburton, whose longstanding interest in science had made him a Fellow of the Royal Society and parliamentary spokesman for the medical profession, demanded an enquiry into the teaching of anatomy. His Select Committee was already sitting by the time Davis and Blundell were fined.

The Committee interviewed leading surgeons, London magistrates, policemen and three anonymous bodysnatchers. It took written reports from Edinburgh and Dublin, and examined the continental system. Altogether it gives us our best over-view of bodysnatching in its heyday, as Naples's diary has left the best intimate picture.

The police estimated that there were no more than ten full-time resurrectionists working in London. (Murphy, Wildes, Hollis, Vaughan and Naples were probably five they had in mind. Davies and Shearman may well have been two more, with one or two of Ike Chapman's men whose names have escaped the records.) On the other hand, nearly 200 part-timers contributed bodies from time to time.

The police quite liked some of the ten professionals. They were steady, decent, quiet and discreet, according to James Glennon and Richard Pople of the Union Hall magistrates' office. The surgeons, on the other hand, detested them. They were 'the lowest dregs of degradation' (Cooper). 'As bad as any in society' (Benjamin Brodie). 'A very bad set of men' (Abernethy). Sir Astley quoted a letter he had received from Joshua Brookes in 1823. Odoriferous Joshua had told him that the full-time bodysnatchers had now become so offensive and insolent that he refused to deal with them, and bought everything he needed from the part-timers and free-lances. The whole system was endangered by four malpractices:

(1) The resurrectionists had started stealing suicides awaiting inquest. This actually involved all of them – receiving surgeons, bodysnatchers and porters alike – in *felony*. (The criminals here were probably Chapman's shadowy gang, who supplied Joshua and specialized in lifting bodies from mortuaries rather than graves.)

(2) Breaking into vaults and tombs caused damage which antagonized wealthy and influential members of the community.

(3) Gang wars with their concomitant quarrels and fights invited detection and attracted public notice and anxiety.

(4) Public concern meant that anatomists were visited almost daily by police officers with search warrants, looking for identified missing cadavers. Brookes had lost three expensive corpses in that way over a month, and he suspected that the bodysnatchers themselves were laying information against their customers, using accomplices to pose as next-of-kin so that they could reclaim cadavers and sell them a second time.

The Committee also heard of poor Joshua's individual sufferings. Once he bought a body in a sack, kicked it down the steps into the basement where he stored subjects awaiting dissection, and then heard noises coming from the sack. Fearing that the bodysnatchers had seized a comatose body in mistake for a corpse, he went down into the basement. He found a man standing beside the empty sack who told him he had been kidnapped while drunk. Brookes doubted this, and kicked him forcefully out of the house. He believed that it was a cunning plot to insinuate a burglar into the Blenheim Steps Academy.

On another occasion, when Brookes refused to buy two subjects, the angry resurrectionists left them openly on the roadway blocking Great Marlborough Street. When they were found, the mob was enraged, and tried to destroy Brookes's house. Not for the first time, he was only saved by the timely arrival of the constables. (William Hunter before him had endured riotous assaults on his anatomy theatre. Wildes once held off an attack on Grainger's Academy until help arrived. And Wakley had his house burnt down because the mob wrongly suspected that he was involved in mutilating or dissecting the corpses of the executed Cato Street conspirators.)

Sir Astley, the richest living surgeon, was also the angriest at the inflation. Subjects had cost two guineas at the outset of his career; now they were eight, and he had once had to pay fourteen. 'The anatomists of London,' he told the Committee, 'were completely at the feet of the resurrection men.' It was all the fault of Crouch:

> . . . who, the moment he was opposed by others, burst into the places in which bodies were contained, and spoiled them for dissection, and did not hesitate to commit burglarious acts for that purpose; or if there was a party of persons disposed to oppose him, he excited a riot against those individuals, and pointed them out as bad characters and as resurrection men; and the magistrates of the Borough were under the necessity very often of settling those differences; the result of which was the present expense of dissection, because it was impossible to compete with a clever fellow, who was also a man of property; and this man therefore had the power of raising the price of subjects as he pleased, and of obliging one lecturer and opposing another.

Sir Astley pointed out that the law in no way hindered him from obtaining any body he wanted; it merely raised the price artificially.

Chairman Warburton, a philosophical radical with an understanding of classical economics, paid little heed to this pretence of a commitment to *laissez faire* submitted by the head of a notorious cartel. To the ultimate fury of the surgeons, he never suggested that an increase of supply to them at a reduced cost should be the main aim of reform.

A less sophisticated committee member put the sympathetic:

> Q. Since [Crouch's] time had not one gang opposing another increased the price?

Even Sir Astley saw the dreadful pitfall of suggesting that competition among sellers could raise the price to the buyer. He gave the evasive:

> A. The possibility of obtaining a supply from London burial grounds is almost destroyed.

Ben Crouch was never named in these exchanges, though there could be no doubt who was intended. And the

Committee was to hear from the great man in person. Under the pseudonym C.D., he emerged from retirement to enlighten the parliamentarians about his life as a bodysnatcher. On the ground that C.D. kept a written record of his takings, previous scholars have claimed that C.D. was Josh Naples referring back to his log-book. But the opening of C.D.'s evidence positively identifies him as Crouch and no other:

> Q. I believe that for several years from 1809 to 1813 you had the sole supply of subjects to the anatomical schools in London?
>
> A. I had.

This rules out pliable Josh, who never had a monopoly of any kind. But 'anatomical schools' being interpreted as anatomy theatres in teaching hospitals, it exactly describes Crouch. He alone expected to supply Bart's, Tommy's and Guy's. The London Hospital supplied itself. And Ike Chapman's market, St George's and the Westminster, farmed out their anatomy classes to Windmill Street: a private dissecting Academy, and not an anatomy school.

C.D.'s testimony is all in the past tense, indicating that he was retired from the business (unlike Naples, who went on sacking-up until 1832). And there is a certain expansiveness about it which indicates that he was enjoying present prosperity. This was probably the period of Crouch's Margate hotel.

His independence and quick temper emerged occasionally. He was still unwilling to offer the emollience with which Naples and Murphy tried to secure the surgeons' goodwill. Why did he stop supplying the schools in 1813?

> A. Why, because there had been trouble with men going out; the lecturers got to supply strange men, and that was the cause of a great deal of trouble.

That had led him to exact a higher price. The profits of bodysnatching were not ample for a man to live on. And it was increasingly dangerous, especially as armed watchmen would now shoot at resurrectionists.

He still had his record books from the days of his monopoly, and they showed that he usually supplied between 350 and 400 subjects a season, of which around 50 would be children's bodies. These were ample for the hospitals' needs: he was usually able to ship some out to Edinburgh or Bristol, and sometimes had unsold subjects left on his hands at the end of the season. (These figures are quite compatible with those that can be calculated from Naples's diary.) Crouch believed that 400 adults and an indeterminate number of 'smalls' would satisfy London's teaching needs.

Exploring every possibility, the Committee wondered whether it might be possible to import bodies from the Continent? Crouch doubted it. There were restrictions laid down by the French and Dutch governments which would probably prevent it. He had never done so himself, though he had, surprisingly, assembled a sort of pre-Hunterian collection of physiological oddities.

> I have imported several curious anatomical specimens, and I have several now, such as separated heads and things of that sort; they are all imported from Paris; I never bought any in the Netherlands.

Bodysnatcher A.B. was still active. He might well have been Murphy, since he came with a testimonial from Brodie's assistant to the effect that he was a full-time bodysnatcher, and one who never laid information against the surgeons; his work was hindered by spoiled graveyards and greedy sextons (so that he cannot have been Ike Chapman or one of his men); he believed himself to be one of the only three full-time and exclusive bodysnatchers in the city; and he was evasive when asked whether he was a gang leader:

> Q. Have you men in your employ for the purpose of raising bodies; that is, would you call yourself the head of a set?
> A. I have worked with one man for seven years.
> Q. Are there other persons who are at the head of parties, employed in raising bodies?
> A. There might be some; but there are many who never supplied the schools and never will.

That last sour reflection on the newcomers to the trade is typical of A.B.'s evidence. Almost admitting his own status,

he remarked that gang leaders informed on each other, and
he would expect six months if arrested. He went on to say
that it was now difficult for a sober man to make a good
living supplying the schools, because of the influx of new
men.

> A great many of them profess to get subjects, that I
> suppose do not get 4 subjects in a year; a great many of
> them that has lately got in the business and have almost
> been the ruin of it.

Ben Crouch, as we saw, was willing to make the robust
accusation that *all* bodysnatchers (except himself) were
thieves. A.B., advertising his own merits and diminishing his
rivals with knocking copy, was more selective. He could not
be Hollis, for he hinted at him in stating that horses and carts
were used for housebreaking. (Constable Glennon would
later confirm that Hollis had been convicted for carrying
housebreaking tools – an extraordinary example of a bodysnatcher's being mentioned by name to this Committee.) He
could not be one of the Spitalfields gang, for he mentioned
them as a body including many of the spurious resurrectionists of the day. His estimate of the numbers relatively
active in the trade seems more realistic than the two hundred
proposed by the police and accepted by the Committee.

> I should suppose there are at present in London between
> 40 and 50 men that have the name of raising subjects, and
> that there is but two more besides myself that get their
> living by it.

If I am right in identifying this witness as Murphy, that last
estimate is probably a discreet testimonial to his continuing
associates, Naples and Wildes. In fact, at this date, I think that
Hollis, Vaughan, Davies and Shearing were also full-time
resurrectionists; and I have no idea who was carrying out the
work of the Chapman gang.

A.B. was consistently sulky about the state of trade. The
newcomers blackmailed the old hands with the threat of
exposure. Sextons needed bribing. London grounds were
unsafe, and he had once been shot at from about two yards
distance. All but two or three of the so-called bodysnatchers

were thieves who lifted a body or two, and then called themselves resurrectionists.

He attributed the inflation to supply and demand. He had once lifted 23 bodies in four nights. In those days they were easy to come by, and the price was only four guineas. He had never kept an account of the numbers taken over the course of a year. Only once, he thought, had he taken more than 100; the following year it had fallen to 50 or 60. (Crouch and Naples alike prove that this was a gross underestimate of a professional gang's output. But it is accurate enough as the number of bodies one member might raise personally.)

Bodysnatcher E.F., a former associate of C.D. (Naples, perhaps), gave a very brief testimony, and it followed a line the surgeons would certainly have liked to see stressed. He said that rich and poor were sacked-up indiscriminately, but the poor, being buried in lighter and shallower graves, were more commonly taken.

The surgeons knew exactly what they wanted. They disagreed with Crouch's estimate of their needs. They had 500 students at any one time engaged in dissection. They received about 450 bodies a year. And they believed that each student should, over a sixteen-month period, work on two subjects to learn the structures of the body, and a third to practise modes of surgical operation. Obviously they needed a far greater supply than currently obtained, and at lower cost.

They wanted to be given all the bodies that were unclaimed after death in prisons, hospitals and workhouses. This was done on the Continent, and they estimated it would supply 1,000 London subjects a year gratis: plenty for their needs. They did not want to receive any more executed murderers, as the notion that dissection was the last and most awful ignominy prejudiced people against anatomy. And, of course, they wanted their own status as scientists and educators raised quite above the perils of the law.

Warburton's Report strongly affirmed the surgeons' case that anatomy was absolutely essential, both as a research instrument to improve methods of healing, and as training for the doctors of the future. It agreed that the supply of bodies should be increased, and argued that this would benefit the poor more than the rich. But it made no recommendation as to how this should be done, and hardly concerned itself with the cost. It endorsed the repeal of the relevant clauses of the 1752 Act Against Murder. It asked Parliament to consider ways of implementing its vague proposals. And it looked as though it didn't really expect any serious action to be taken.

Events in Scotland were to prove far more important than the surgeons' professional advice in activating legislative reform.

SIX

The Golden Age
in Scotland

Scottish bodysnatching stayed essentially in the hands of students and junior doctors until 1819. Thereafter it was still only in Edinburgh that professional resurrectionists came to the fore, as it was only in Edinburgh that competition between surgeons raised prices sufficiently to make a viable market. Barclay and Monro avoided open confrontation and sent their students and assistants to fetch bodies from different parts of the town. But their two most brilliant pupils changed the whole situation.

Robert Liston came up to Edinburgh University in 1808. He was a strong, active young man and a fine sportsman. In later years he would become a great figure in yachting circles. In his youth, he was an amateur boxer who attracted the attention of the fancy.

To young Liston, surgery was a practical matter of skill and dexterity, while bodysnatching was fine nocturnal sport. His strength and agility made him a notably rapid operator. He was described as the finest surgeon in Europe, by which was meant the quickest and most accurate. He could amputate a leg in 28 seconds, though once, in achieving this feat, he accidentally amputated two of his assistant's fingers and the patient's left testicle as well. He became Barclay's assistant, and served him until 1816. Then, to broaden his experience, he went to London for two years' study.

As a boxer and surgeon, he met Ben Crouch. Unlike the English practitioners, he found the great resurrectionist wonderful company. And their acquaintance coincided perfectly with Crouch's being pensioned off from bodysnatching in London.

The year 1818 found Liston preparing to return to Edinburgh to open his own School of Surgery. It found Crouch at a loose end, freed from prison after the St Albans rumpus. In an inspired moment, the 24-year-old surgeon put Ben Crouch on his pay-roll as an Instructor in Bodysnatching.

Crouch and Liston became the greatest bodysnatching team in Scottish history. They smashed through the gentlemen's agreement maintained by Barclay and Monro, taking bodies wherever they fancied, and forcing the other young gentlemen from Surgeon's Square and the University to do likewise. It led to confrontation, of course. And Crouch and Liston did not always come off victorious. Robert Christison served his internship at the Infirmary during the exciting years 1817–20, and undoubtedly participated keenly in the bodysnatching exploits of the time. But as a distinguished Professor of Medical Jurisprudence when he compiled his memoirs, he preferred to describe the illegal adventures of a less illustrious contemporary.

> Mowbray Thomson had a risky encounter in this way. Though his assistantship with Dr. Barclay necessarily ceased on his becoming an Infirmary Resident, he had so great a passion for adventure, that he used to drop from his window, scale the city wall which then bounded the hospital grounds to the south, and join his companions in their unholy occupation. On the occasion referred to, he was perched on the churchyard wall as sentinel, when Liston hove in view with his assistants, and a notorious London resurrectionist, Crouch, who had made the metropolis too hot for him, and had been taken into Liston's pay as an instructor during his rustication in Edinburgh. Thomson jumped into the burying-ground, sat down across the grave, stuck his digger into it, and when

the intruders followed him, claimed the grave as his. Liston and Crouch first jeered at him, and then threatened to remove him by force. But, as they drew near for the purpose, he presented a pistol in the face of the foremost, and swore he would defend himself to the uttermost. More altercation ensued, during which succour to the weaker party arrived in the shape of Thomson's companions. A general row appeared imminent, but Liston thought better of it, and left the enemy in undisturbed possession of their claim.

More commonly, Liston and Crouch carried all before them. According to Henry Lonsdale, the assistant of his great rival, Knox, Liston was:

> . . . a Napier in action, bold, dexterous, aye ready, and in the van of danger, and single-handed equal to any three of the regular staff of workmen. Thus one night when a party of medicals headed by this surgeon saw that they were discovered in a city churchyard, the chief actor laid hold of two large "adults" that moment disinterred, and, carrying one under each arm, escaped by a door which led into the garden of a private institution. Perhaps no man in Edinburgh could have done such a feat of strength, or made so good a retreat whilst under "the cover" of blunderbusses.

Inevitably, the intrusion of this team into the uncompetitive world of Barclay and Monro forced their students to start fighting each other. Cullen's grandson, himself to become a prominent surgeon, studied under Barclay and led a team of student resurrectionists. When a crippled ballad singer named Sandie M'Nab died in the Infirmary, young Cullen led his fellows to the burial ground, disinterred and boxed the body, and left it under a high window of Barclay's, which overlooked the cemetery, while the party went up to fix ropes and pulleys for its removal. No sooner were they out of the grounds than a gang of Monro's students turned up, seized the box, and started lifting it over the wall. Cullen and his friends rushed out, and a long fight ensued which attracted the watch. The University lads fled on hearing authority approach, and Cullen was able to haul M'Nab's body up to Barclay's rooms.

Bodysnatching could play a strange part in more personal rivalry. Around 1818, Henry Ferguson and George Duncan were medical students lodging together in Potterow. Both fell in love with a Miss Wilson of Bruntsfield Links, who would not declare her preference, so that the room-mates' friendship turned to jealousy and hatred of each other. Before the triangle could be resolved, Ferguson contracted a baffling disease and died. His body was, of course, anatomically desirable, and Duncan, having seen him buried by day, collected a professional bodysnatcher known as 'the Screw' ('from the adroit way in which he managed the extracting instrument') to sack him up by night. What should the young man find at the graveside but Miss Wilson, sobbing her heart out for 'Dear Henry'.

As soon as she left, Duncan turned to his resurrectionism with a zest, and for the remainder of his student days he delighted in passing bright moonlit nights watching from a distance as Miss Wilson wept and prayed at the grave, and gloating over the fact that she was wasting her emotions on empty soil.

Successive rows in the city attracted public attention and increased the number of watchmen and mortsafes in the graveyards. Liston and Crouch thereupon turned their attention to the villages along the Forth, which Liston's skill as a boatman brought within their reach. They were witness to a sad romantic scene at Rosyth by Limekilns when they went to fetch the body of a recently drowned sailor. His sweetheart was weeping at the graveside in the moonlight when they arrived. After a while she strewed flowers on the grave and moved away. The bodysnatchers hastily dug up the body. One of them took a flower for his buttonhole, and they lugged the sack back down to the beach. As they were pushing their boat out, the girl returned and found the grave disturbed. She cried desperately, ran down to the beach, and gave a heart-rending scream when she saw the oars strike and the little boat move out of her reach. As a professional surgeon, Liston was sure he had been right to keep the body. But he always confessed that the girl's distress had pained him more than any operation he carried out.

These romantic moments in Scotland show that Caledonian bodysnatchers were less perturbed by moonlight than Josh Naples in London. In the countryside, at least, this was because the watchmen were pretty careless. They arrived well after nightfall, leaving the first hour of darkness available for bodysnatching. They slipped off to taverns when they should have been on guard. One of them, notoriously, did nothing more than fire a gun across the graveyard every half-hour without even looking at it.

Liston and Crouch dressed in sailors' clothes when they took their boat to Cures to collect the victim of an unusual disease. Once it was in the sack, they hid it under a hedge while they went to an inn to pass the night before sailing home. A very pretty barmaid they called Mary was in charge, and they had the inn to themselves. Liston was soon flirting merrily with Mary, when a cry of 'Ahoy!' from outside interrupted his tender passages. Mary leaped up and flung open the door for her sailor brother, who swung in, carrying, to Crouch and Liston's horror, the sack they had left under the hedge. Fortunately he didn't recognize them. He had simply seen two men hide a bundle furtively and make off into the night. He assumed they were thieves, and he swung the sack down on the floor, saying: 'There, and if it ain't something good, rot them chaps there who stole it!'

The bodysnatchers watched with frozen anxiety as he took his knife and cut the sack open. It was the sailor's turn to freeze when the body fell out; in a moment, with cries of revulsion, he and his sister rushed out of the room. Crouch and Liston abandoned all thoughts of sleep, grabbed their subject, and raced for the boat to sail away in the darkness.

Their most famous exploit was the collection of a body with a hydrocephalic head. This had been buried by the Forth, and it was well known that Liston, Monro and Barclay all coveted it. An unusually strict watch was set in consequence. Realizing that the bodysnatchers were succeeding in taking corpses before the watchmen arrived, the relatives had guards posted the instant darkness fell. Every party that went out found the graveyard manned against them. Liston and Crouch, therefore, abandoned their boat and hired a gig.

Dressed as gentlemen, they went out to the village and took tea at the inn during the afternoon. Then, leaving their gig in the stables, they went for a stroll while it was still daylight. They had not been gone more than half an hour, when a pock-marked servant in red livery arrived at the inn with a bundle which he said his master wanted left for the gentlemen. He was shown to the gig, where he packed it away, and then left. Soon afterwards, the two gentlemen strolled back, boarded their vehicle, and drove off in the dusk.

As they climbed in, the stable-boy caught a flash of red under one of the gentlemen's cloaks, and he remarked to the ostler that the second gentleman looked very like the servant who had brought the bundle.

'Haud yer tongue, Sandie! Ye're aye seeing farlies,' snapped the ostler.

This disinterment in half an hour by daylight was one of the most remarkable feats of all resurrectionism. The skeleton was presented to the College of Surgeons, numbered 3,489, and proudly ticketed with Liston's name as donor.

Lonsdale, the passionate admirer of a man who despised Liston, nonetheless confessed:

> Two such accomplished artists in their own line as Liston, the Edinburgh surgeon, and Crouch, the London Resurrectionist, the world never saw before, and, now that "Othello's occupation's gone," cannot possibly see again.

Being trained by Crouch, the Scottish doctors knew just how bodysnatching was done. The general public believed that the coffin was uncovered and heaved to the surface with gimlets and ropes. (Dickens describes such a scene in *A Tale of Two Cities* and Phiz illustrated one for a book of true crimes.) The London surgeons knew this was untrue; raising coffins was far too slow, and they only came to the surface when graveyards were spoiled. The resurrectionists put about an extraordinary story to the effect that they normally dug an eighteen-inch square tunnel from outside the grave to the head of the coffin; knocked away the narrow side adjacent to the cranium; folded the corpse's shoulders over its chest, and dragged the body out with a rope. This had the supposed advantage of leaving the grave undisturbed.

In fact, as Josh Naples admitted once the trade was over, the description was a complete scam, invented in the hope that any enthusiastic amateurs among doctors and students would try it and give up bodysnatching in despair. The unturned soil of the 'tunnel' would have taken an age to excavate; its opening would have been obvious amid the undisturbed turf; and the engineering skill involved in leading the tunnel's inner end to the coffin's head was unlikely to emerge from frenzied, illicit digging in the dark.

Sir Robert Christison, who had clearly done it himself, coyly ascribed his account of bodysnatching to:

> The resurrectionists in Edinburgh . . . chiefly the assistants of the several teachers of anatomy. With them I was well acquainted; so that I came to know the whole process . . . .
>
> A hole was dug down to the coffin only to where the head lay – a canvas sheet being stretched around to receive the earth, and to prevent any of it spoiling the smooth uniformity of the grass. The digging was done with short, flat, dagger-shaped implements of wood, to avoid the clicking noise of iron striking stones. On reaching the coffin, two broad iron hooks under the lid, pulled forcibly up with a rope, broke off a sufficient portion of the lid to allow the body to be dragged out; and sacking was heaped over the whole to deaden the sound of cracking wood. The body was stripped of the grave-clothes, which were scrupulously buried again; it was secured in a sack; and the surface of the ground was restored to its original condition, – which was not difficult, as the sod over a fresh-filled grave must always present signs of recent disturbance. The whole process could be completed in an hour, even though the grave might be six feet deep, because the soil was loose, and the digging was done impetuously by frequent relays of active men.

The estimate of an hour to complete the snatch proves this to be a first-hand amateur account. Liston and Crouch – two men rather than relays – took half an hour to raise the hydrocephalic. The best teams could have a body sacked up in a quarter of an hour if the grave were shallow. But they admitted that it was the hardest physical work any experienced manual labourer might ever undertake.

Liston's students followed him to the country in pursuit of cadavers. They proved, perhaps, the worst bodysnatchers of all time. One team at Rosythe hastening away from an approaching figure with a dog and a lantern, caught their subject's head on a rubble bank, scalping her, and leaving the ghastly trophy of her long black hair to be discovered by her widower. Another, at Gilmerton, abandoned their whole subject in the middle of the road, so that the young farmer who had been married to her imagined his unhappy wife had been buried alive and risen from the grave, until a carrier from Penycuik relieved his feelings by suggesting disturbed body-snatchers. The reason for her being dropped was that the students had failed to bring a sack with them, and gave her to the tallest of their number to carry on his back, with her arms flung over his shoulders. As they hurried away they became increasingly nervous, and their pace rose from a march to a trot. The subject slipped a little down her carrier's back, until her feet touched the ground, and she bounced along with awkward leaps and hops. With a cry of, 'She's alive!' the terrified student dropped her in the road, and fled pell-mell with his companions.

Shortly after Crouch retired from his Instructorship, Dr Robert Knox came back to the city of his birth. Three years older than Liston, he had been the most brilliant pupil at Edinburgh Academy and the most brilliant student at the University, twice elected President of the Royal Medical Society before graduating. He failed anatomy under Monro, took Barclay's classes to make up, and gained a positive passion for human and comparative anatomy as a key to the nature of life.

Once qualified, he joined the army as a surgeon and practised at Waterloo. With Napoleon's defeat he took half-pay, and continued his anatomical studies in South Africa and Paris. He became accustomed to the French practice of dissecting unburied corpses taken from hospitals, and strongly approved of the system which supplied fresh subjects by handing terminal patients over to surgeons if they were unclaimed. He was a deist (or agnostic), a free-thinking rationalist, mildly pro-revolutionary, and definitely an advanced intellectual. When he came back to Edinburgh to help place part of Sir Charles Bell's anatomy collection in the museum, he was plainly the best scientist among the city's dissectors. Barclay shared his intellectual grasp and passion, but his mind was ageing while Knox's was in its prime.

Monro III's incompetence coincided with increased demands that students demonstrate proficiency in dissection. Private anatomy schools, therefore, started to flourish. In addition to Liston's establishment, the Lizars brothers pioneered teaching from brilliantly coloured diagrams, painter William illustrating surgeon John's preparation. Young Cullen and Henry Syme worked with Liston, and took over his teaching when he finally decided to concentrate exclusively on his practice. Knox began to help Barclay with his lectures ; entered partnership with him in 1825 ; and took over the school at 10 Surgeon's Square when the old man died in 1826.

Knox's brilliance attracted students in ever-increasing numbers. Barclay had lectured to 200 in a course. Knox increased this to 350 before the old man's death, and in 1829 accepted 500 students : the largest anatomy class ever seen in Britain.

He was ugly, his face disfigured by smallpox in infancy, which had been so severe as to blind his left eye, leaving it a grey-green blank like a sightless grape. But he dressed nattily, lecturing in perfectly cut, plum-coloured coats. And his voice was musical, his address winning and his range of interests fascinating. He was a delightful host to his students, and encouraged them to discuss philosophy, theology, literature and music at his dinner table. (His own favourites were Cervantes, Shakespeare, the Bible, Handel, Schubert and Rossini.)

Fellow-surgeons tended to avoid his social company. They felt that he married beneath his station in 1824, though he circumvented this social difficulty by using his sister, Mary, as a formal hostess, while enjoying a happy married life in private. They also had to endure the biting sarcasm with which he entered the professional competition. His discipular students felt a vicarious superiority to the other heads of the profession when they adopted their master's views. One recorded an attack on Liston with which he opened a lecture :

> Before commencing today's lecture, I am compelled by the
> sacred calls of duty to notice an extraordinary surgical
> operation which has this morning been performed in a
> neighbouring building by a gentleman who, I believe,
> regards himself as the first surgeon in Europe. A country
> labourer from Tranent came to the infirmary a few days
> ago with an aneurism of considerable extent, connected
> with one of the large arteries of the neck ; and
> notwithstanding its being obvious to the merest tyro that it
> *was* an aneurism, the most distinguished surgeon in
> Europe, after an apparently searching examination,
> pronounced it to be an abscess. Accordingly, this
> professional celebrity – who among other things plumes
> himself upon the wonderful strength of his hands and
> arms, without pretension to head, and is an amateur
> member of the ring – plunged his knife into what he
> foolishly imagined to be an abscess ; and the blood
> bursting forth from the deep gash in the aneurismal sac, the
> patient was dead in a few seconds . . . . It is surely
> unnecessary for me to add that a knowledge of anatomy,
> physiology, pathology and surgery, is neither connected
> with nor dependent upon brute force, ignorance and
> presumption.

Rough stuff, but not misplaced. Liston could take care of
himself. And the students were forcefully reminded that
accurate diagnosis before an operation mattered as much as
skilful surgery.

It might seem that snobbery over his wife and professional
jealousy explained the University's unwillingness to make
Knox a lecturer. But Knox had one devastating failing that
justified his colleagues in ostracizing him. According to his
devoted pupil, Henry Lonsdale, with many virtues of
kindness, generosity and tenderness, he nonetheless tended to
be evasive about matters of business principle, and to
exaggerate and prevaricate, especially about personalities. In
plain English, he told malicious and self-interested lies to
other people's detriment. This truly devilish failing – the
crime of Iago – left him deservedly friendless when he

urgently needed professional support.

Knox's contribution to Edinburgh bodysnatching was in keeping with his cerebral approach to surgery. He did not accompany bodysnatchers himself, and he did not encourage his students and assistants to go out robbing graveyards. He agitated for an introduction of the continental system (in which his colleagues agreed with him) and he bought cadavers from professionals. He spent lavishly to provide his students with an ample supply of subjects. In one season he spent between £700 and £800 on bodies alone. At a time of shortage he paid the astonishing sum of twenty guineas for a single cadaver. He enlarged the demand, and the market responded by engendering professionals to produce the supply.

Imports from England and Ireland were part of the trade. Loftus's coaches sent Yorkshire bodies up to Edinburgh. The Henderson gang despatched them from Liverpool. The London resurrectionists sold surpluses to Scotland. The quays were filled with boxes from Dublin purporting to be cured pork, stuffed animals, dry-salted beef, even blacking or apples. Many were so badly packed that they stank on arrival or even before shipping, and they were impounded by customs in Edinburgh and Dublin.

Bodies could not be sent at cash-on-delivery terms ; the surgeons had to settle up through agents. One young Irish doctor, known as 'The Captain', took to sacking-up his own terminal patients, despatching them to Edinburgh, and making rare visits to Scotland to collect the moneys accrued. He was a macabre, jovial man, who made broad jests about his subjects at dinners given in his honour. Once he saw one of his former patients lying in a dissecting room, and apostrophized her thus for the benefit of his hosts :

> Ah, Mistress O'Neil ! did I spare the whisky on you,
> which you loved so well, – and didn't you lave me a purty
> little sum to keep the resurrectionists away from you, – and
> didn't I take care of you myself ? And by Jesus you are
> there, and don't thank me for coming to see you.

Punctilious payment was important to keep the Dublin trade going, and despite his evasiveness in business, Knox had an excellent reputation in this respect. In the season of

1828–9, Syme was forced to cancel his anatomy class for lack of subjects, and he left several ordered but unpaid for. The Dublin agent wrote upbraiding him, and remarking : 'Knox's word once passed I have never known him to violate . . . . Knox is honourable in all his transactions.'

Knox's incursion into the market also coincided – not accidentally, one infers – with the emergence of the only professional Scottish gang to compare with the London resurrectionists. This was headed by Andrew Lees or Merrilees, a country carter whose house overlooked a church-yard. His trade was an excellent cover for delivering boxes to Edinburgh, and he robbed the graves next door freely for some time. But he drank sixteen glasses of whisky a day, and eventually gave himself away by boasting in his cups. He was forced to sell up, move to Edinburgh, and become a full-time bodysnatcher. Still, when prices rose, he took to going back to the old graveyard where, he claimed, he could get bodies, 'as cheaply as penny pies'.

It seems that he was extremely tall and so disproportionately thin that he found it impossible to find clothes to fit him. His lantern-jawed face was pulled deliberately into exaggerated expressions and grimaces, though these may have been very effective when he dressed in black and followed funerals, simulating grief. His conversation was accompanied by gawky, loose-limbed gesticulations, and students found him so grotesque that they adapted his name to the soubriquet 'Merry Andrew' – the generic clown's name of travelling zanies.

His chief associates were 'The Spune' (Spoon), and 'Moudiewarp' (Mole) Mowatt : the one nicknamed after his curiously-shaped spade, and the other for his digging prow-ess.

Spune was a short, stout, clean-shaven man, with the air of a threadbare Methodist minister. He prided himself on being a humble contributor to the progress of science, which his student customers found inordinately funny, though it was obviously true. He had some self-education, and could use the Latin names for parts of the body when discussing his clients' requirements. Withal, he seems to have been a little self-righteous.

Mowatt was a drunken plasterer with no intellectual pretensions whatever. (Merry Andrew picked up a few Latin words from Spune.) He was simply a hard and fast excavator.

A fourth associate, known as 'Praying Howard', habitually wore a black suit and white choker, and was given to bursts of extempore prayer at funerals. Altogether this gang seems to have been over-burdened with lugubrious pseudo-mourners.

Like Crouch and Murphy, Merrilees was accused of dividing the takings unfairly. This had led to a rift in the gang when his sister died at Penycuik. Spune and Mowatt decided that they would reimburse themselves at the family's expense after she was buried, and they hired a cart from David Cameron to fetch the body back to Edinburgh. Cameron mentioned to Merrilees that his gang was off to the country that night, and Andrew guessed what was afoot. Armed with a white sheet, he made his way to the graveyard before his associates, and as soon as they had the body on the grass before them, he donned the sheet and rose from behind a gravestone with eldritch howls and threatening gestures. Spune and Mowatt fled from the bogle.

Then Andrew spoke for the last time to his lifeless sister.

'And you're there, Sarah Merrilees?' he said. 'The Spune's without its porridge this time. And shall not man live on the fruit of the earth?'

With which, he bundled her up, and made for the roadway. In the distance he saw Spune and Mowatt leading Cameron's horse and cart away. Hurrying after them, he started to shout 'Robbers!' while they were at too great a distance to recognize him. And, as he had hoped, they ran, leaving him the transportation to carry his sister back to Surgeon's Square.

Andrew himself was the victim of a celebrated deception, however. A student saw him lurking at the corner of a wynd one night, and guessing that he was waiting for a poor slum-dweller to die, whispered in his ear, 'She's dead.'

Andrew raced into a tenement, and called out to the old nurse who had tended the dying woman, 'It's all ower, I hear. And when will we come for the body?'

'Whisht, ye mongrel!' snapped the nurse. 'She's lively as a cricket!'

This sinister conversation, overheard by the unhappy patient, had two consequences. The patient suffered a relapse and died the following night. And the nurse suffered a fit of conscience about selling her body. When Andrew returned, hoping to complete the sale, she refused to treat with him.

'A light has come doon upon me frae heaven,' she told him, 'and I canna.'

'Light frae heaven !' grated the bodysnatcher ; 'Will that shew the doctors how to cut a cancer out o' ye, ye auld fule ? But we'll sune put out that light.'

Spune, who accompanied him, went out to fetch a bottle of whisky, remarking (according to the Edinburgh journalist who investigated the men's doings) : 'Ay, we are only obeying the will of God. Man's infirmities shall verily be cured by the light of His wisdom. I forget the text.'

On his return, Andrew poured the old lady a stiff tot, saying : 'Tak' ye that, and it will drive the devil out o' ye.'

After her second glass, he took out a pound note, held it up to the candle, and said : 'And now, look through that, ye auld devil, and ye'll see some o' the real light o' heaven that will make your cat's een reel.'

The nurse's conscience dissolved in whisky. Her business instincts did not. 'But that's only ane,' she complained, 'and ye ken ye promised three.'

'And here they are.'

'Weel, ye may take her.'

At this unpropitious moment, a stranger wearing a great-coat and huge cravat, much of his face covered by a broad bonnet, made his way into the room. He was nephew to the deceased, he announced, and he wished to see her body with a view to arranging its burial. Spune and Andrew beat a hasty retreat, pursued for some distance by the indignant 'nephew'. Who was, in reality, the very student who had set up the prank in the first place.

Sir Robert Christison claimed that the authorities recognized the importance of anatomy, and quietly ensured that nobody was ever arrested for bodysnatching in Scotland. The only case I have found going through the Edinburgh courts was that of a man named Wight (could he have been 'White', the Scot who corrupted Josh Naples ?) taken in 1811 for replacing a Canongate neighbour's body with sand as it lay in the house awaiting burial. Consequently, stories of Scottish bodysnatching are anecdotal reminiscences, unsupported by manuscript documentation or sworn statements. There can be no doubt that Andrew Merrilees, Spune, Mowatt and Howard existed and practised resurrectionism. But there is no reliable testimony to confirm their adventures. I trust Lonsdale's account of Merrilees' origins. There is no question about his communication with Knox's man on the night when Burke and Hare offered their final subject. But I fear that the two longer stories of the gang were, at the very least, embellished by the lively imagination of Alexander Leighton, when he collected old men's reminiscences of the great days of bodysnatching.

The end of those days was firmly heralded on 29 November 1827, when two short, furtive Irishmen appeared in the University asking for Professor Monro's men, and explaining (perfectly truthfully) that they could bring the body of a man who had just died of dropsy at their house, should the professor want it. The student they accosted cared about science, and he told Burke and Hare it would be better to sell the body to Dr Robert Knox at 10 Surgeon's Square.

SEVEN

Burke and Hare

William Roughead, in his *Famous Trials* volume on Burke and Hare, is understandably facetious at the expense of Henry Cockburn's tactless exception:

> Except that he murdered, Burke was a sensible, and what might be called a respectable man; not at all ferocious in his general manner, sober, correct in all his other habits.

But Cockburn was a great lawyer and no fool. As the most prominent counsel in the defence team he had occasion to observe Burke closely at his trial. His remarks are judicious, though oxymoronic. William Burke seems to be a terrible instance of a decent man falling swiftly to temptation and corruption.

He was born in Orrey, Co. Tyrone, in 1792. As a clean and apt schoolboy, he was a credit to his respectable peasant parents. His first employment was in the service of a Presbyterian minister, and he retained an interest in the protestant theology of grace and salvation. He worked briefly as a weaver and a baker, and then followed his brother Constantine into the Donegal militia. He played the fife in the company band, and for the rest of his life was a popular flautist, playing and singing Irish ballads with great effect and apparent sensitivity.

He married a woman from Ballinho, Co. Mayo, and they had two children. When the militia disbanded, he wanted to join her family as a smallholder, sub-leasing land from his father-in-law. But there was a family row in which Mrs Burke apparently took her father's side. Burke emigrated to Scotland to work as a navvy on the Union Canal from Glasgow to Edinburgh. He wrote to his wife, asking her and the children to join him, but she never replied. He never saw or heard from her again.

In about 1818, Burke met Helen M'Dougal from Maddiston, Muiravonside, Stirling. She had been born Helen Dougal; carried a child for a married neighbour called M'Dougal, and lived with him after his wife died. When he himself died, she may have supported herself by prostitution among the canal builders. But she quickly settled to living with Burke, and remained faithful to him.

Journalists, eager to damn Burke completely, asserted that he treated her abominably, introducing other women into bed with her and beating her savagely when she objected. It seems clear that Burke had a roving eye. But in other respects, we may prefer Helen M'Dougal's statement to a chap-book author who interviewed her and Burke, and was obviously more their kind of person than the educated gentlemen of the Edinburgh press. Helen was quite insistent that Burke had always been an excellent husband.

After the canal was finished, the Burkes came to Edinburgh and settled in a famous slum lodging-house, Mikey Culzean's 'Beggar's Hotel'. Burke was hawking old clothes, skins and hair. When Culzean's burned down, Burke lost a little library of devotional books, including *The Pilgrim's Progress*, and the works of several Presbyterian divines. He moved with Mikey to a new 'Beggar's Hotel' in Grassmarket, where he devoutly attended prayer meetings at the house next door. At this period, he was described as:

> Kind and serviceable, inoffensive and playful . . .
> industrious as well, and seldom inclined for drink . . . . All
> of which qualities were combined with a jocular and
> quizzical turn, which, displaying a fund of low humour,
> made him a favourite.

His decline began when he left Culzean's and went to
Peebles as a roadmender. In rough company, he took to
drinking heavily at weekends, and fighting when drunk. He
went to Penycuik for the harvest of 1827, and in the autumn
returned to Edinburgh, going to an Irish accommodation-
house in West Port that rivalled Culzean's: Log's Lodgings.

Log or Logue had also come to work on the Union Canal,
but as a sub-contractor rather than a day-labourer. He
worked alongside his men, and his tough, thrifty wife,
Margaret Laird, wore a man's coat and pushed a wheelbarrow
alongside him. Though she ruled him in the house, she was a
first-rate business partner, and when the canal was finished,
the two came to Edinburgh and put their savings into renting
the ground floor of a house at the bottom of Tanner's Close,
West Portsburgh. It had two large rooms, with a small ten
foot by five foot space behind them that could be closed off
and bolted from inside. It also had the use of a stable or pigsty
in the adjoining wall of the close. Log put three or four beds
in each of the large rooms, and let them to the poor, sleeping
two or three to a bed.

In about 1825 he died, and Margaret started to sleep with a
good-looking young lodger. In 1827, a lodger who had been
thrown out previously by Log returned, and Margaret
transferred her affections to him.

Yet another Irish immigrant navvy, William Hare had
continued to work on the canal, loading barges after it was
finished. From that he moved to hawking fish and scrap from
a horse and cart, though his business had declined to handcart
level by the time Margaret Laird took him into her bed. He
was happy to become a lodging-house manager and look after
some pigs in the sty. And he was happy to let William Burke
have the use of the little space at the back of the house for the
cobbling business he had recently taken up.

Hare persistently received a worse press than Burke. This
was partly because he escaped punishment by turning King's
Evidence. Partly, too, because he was physically stronger and
by all accounts more brutal than Burke. But mostly because
he was cursed with a fixed smirking simper, and burst into
nervous giggling when disconcerted. As long as he was plain
William Hare the lodging-house keeper, this was mere self-

effacing Irish charm. But once he was William Hare the murderer it became heartless mockery of the memory of his victims; leering and gloating at the thought of murder and money.

Fortunately, every artist who sketched him during the trials caught the expression perfectly, and we can see at once that it was exasperating and vacuous, but not malign.

Very shortly after Burke moved into Log's, an old pensioner named Desmond came down with dropsy. A few days before his pension fell due he died, to Hare's chagrin. He owed the lodging-house £4 rent, and now it would never be collected. Burke, working indoors at his new trade of patching discarded shoes with scraps of leather before taking them out to sell on the streets, had become friends with his landlord. One of the two had the idea that Desmond's body might be sold to the surgeons to recoup the debt. When the parish officers nailed the old man up in a pauper's coffin, Hare broke it open; Burke lifted out the body; and Hare stuffed the coffin with tanner's bark.

They learned two lessons from their first sale. The surgeons did not want clothes deliverd with bodies (Knox's assistants quickly removed Desmond's feloniously taken shirt and handed it back to the bodysnatchers). And a single body was worth a great deal of money. Dr Knox himself valued this one at £7 10s., and it was evidently not a perfect specimen.

Burke and Hare made separate confessions after Burke's conviction. They listed the same number of victims, but put them in different orders, and the Edinburgh *Evening Courant*, which published an amplification of Burke's confession, gave yet a third and quite different order. Hare's is now lost, but Sir Walter Scott, who examined it, observed that it was most likely correct in suggestion that the first subject the two murdered was a miller called Joseph. Like Desmond, he fell ill while lodging at Log's, and a pillow was used to suffocate him – a practice which they soon abandoned.

One feature of his murder was to be repeated. Joseph was a heavy drinker, and Burke and Hare shared convivial drams with him before killing him. This had the twin advantages of rendering him speechless (in his case, as much a matter of his illness as the alcohol) and of giving them Dutch courage. Burke, Hare and their victims were generally drunk for the murders. Joseph's body fetched £10.

Another sick lodger was an Englishman with jaundice. He came from Cheshire and sold matches on the Edinburgh streets, though Burke did not know his name. He was suffocated by the method the two came to prefer: one lay across his body to hold him down while the other used his hands to seal the victim's nose and mouth.

This mode of killing was probably first used on old Abigail Simpson of Gilmerton, a salt-pedlar who came to Edinburgh once a month to receive the charitable donation of 1s.6d. and a can of dripping from a gentleman's housekeeper. Hare found her on the streets and invited her to spend the night at Log's. They drank away her 1s.6d.; Hare bought the dripping for a further 1s.6d.; and they drank that away. He was very jolly when the old woman said she had a daughter. He promised to marry the daughter and bring 'all the money' into the family. The Hares and Burkes put Mrs Simpson to bed in Burke's little back room when drink overcame her. In the morning, she was very hung over and cried for her daughter. The two murderers gave her stout and whisky to soothe her before killing her. Knox's assistants sent a porter to help carry the body, and Knox himself approved of its freshness when he came to inspect it. By now the pair were on his books as the acknowledged bodysnatchers 'John and William'. Old Abigail's daughter became a familiar figure on the Edinburgh streets over the next few months, enquiring anxiously for her mother.

Another old woman's murder comes down to us in two completely different accounts, both supposedly emanating from Burke. He confessed to George Tait the Sheriff-Substitute that a drunken old woman whose name he did not know lodged one night at Log's in May, and incapacited herself further with drink the following day while he was alone in the house with her. So he killed her, all on his own, and the pair sold her to Knox as usual.

But the *Evening Courant* was told that Margaret Laird decoyed her into the house while Hare was working on the canal-boats, and plied her with drink three times until she fell asleep. Then, on Hare's return, *he* smothered her with bed-ticking while Burke was busy mending shoes. If the murderers confused and forgot one murder apiece, or tried to conceal their solo activities from each other, it may just be that Burke and Hare killed seventeen people rather than the sixteen with which history credits them. Certainly, as John Wilson, Edinburgh's second-rate philosophy professor but first-rate journalist, had Hogg, 'the Ettrick Shepherd', remark in an imaginary dialogue in *Blackwood's Magazine*, there was a dull repetitiveness about the murders:

> First ae drunk auld wife, then anither drunk auld wife –
> and then a third drunk auld wife – and then a drunk auld or
> sick man or twa. The confusion got unco monotonous –
> the Lights and Shadows o' Scottish Death want relief –
> though, to be sure, poor Peggy Paterson, that Unfortunate,
> broke in a little on the uniformity.

Mary Paterson or Mitchell was killed in April 1828. She was an eighteen-year-old orphan who had taken to whoring in the company of Janet Brown. They lodged, first with Mrs Lawrie in Canongate and then with Mrs Worthington nearby. These 'landladies' were probably bawds.

On 8 April both girls were arrested – probably for drunkenness – and held overnight in Canongate watch-house. Next morning they were released and went for some whisky to William Swanston's rum-shop. They saw Burke drinking rum with Swanston, who furiously denied Janet's later claim that he was chatting amiably with his customer. Burke spied the girls, bought them rum, and invited them back to 'his lodgings' for breakfast, saying he would 'keep them handsomely and make them comfortable for life'. Mary came willingly; Janet less so; and Burke generously gave each of them a bottle of whisky.

He took them to his brother Constantine's apartment – a single room in Gibb's Close, Canongate. Constantine had brought his wife and children to Edinburgh where he was a street-cleaner. But Burke pretended to be an unrelated lodger, and abused his sister-in-law Elizabeth for not having laid breakfast. It was a handsome meal of eggs, tea, bread and Finnan haddocks when it came. Mary ate gratefully, supped her whisky, and passed out on the table. Janet remained woozy but capable, and Burke suggested a walk in the fresh air to clear her head.

The walk led them to another shop, where he bought her pies and porter, after which they returned to Gibb's Close. Mary was now fast asleep on one of the two beds in the room. The other was hung with tattered curtains, and Burke was trying to persuade Janet to join him in it when the curtains parted, and Helen M'Dougal's head popped out, bawling curses at Janet for seducing her husband and Burke for bringing a whore home. Husband and wife quarrelled passionately until Burke threw a glass at Helen, cutting her forehead, and pushed her out into the passage, locking the door against her. Elizabeth ran away to fetch help. Mary slept peacefully through the rumpus.

Burke tried again to persuade Janet into bed, but Helen screeching at the door distracted the girl, who insisted on leaving. Burke shepherded her past the harpy on the landing, and she made her way to Mrs Lawrie's house, arriving at 10.00 a.m. Her former protector didn't like the sound of the whole business and sent Janet back to Gibb's Close with a maid to fetch Mary away immediately.

It took the fuddled Janet twenty minutes to find the place again, and when she arrived, Burke had left. The Hares were there, and Mrs Hare stopped Helen M'Dougal from springing on Janet and tearing her face. Hare told Janet that Mary had gone out with Burke, and would be back soon. He invited Janet to have a drink with them while she waited, and despite Helen's continued cursing, she accepted, sending the maid back to tell Mrs Lawrie what was going on. Mrs Lawrie still disliked the situation, and the maid rapidly returned to take Janet away. And all the time, Mary lay dead behind the bed curtains and Burke was in Surgeon's Square arranging her sale.

Janet, Mrs Lawrie and Mrs Worthington were all deeply suspicious when Mary never reappeared. From time to time Janet saw Constantine on the streets, and asked him if he had heard from her. Once he said: 'How the hell can I tell about you sorts of folk? You are here today and away tomorrow.' Another time he told her: 'I am often out upon my lawful business, and how can I answer for all that takes place in my house in my absence?' The law could never prove anything against even Helen M'Dougal and Margaret Laird. But the records clearly suggest that they were active members of the gang, and Constantine and Elizabeth Burke occasional assistants and beneficiaries.

Mrs Lawrie, Mrs Worthington and Janet Brown urgently wanted an enquiry into Mary Paterson's disappearance. But their occupation precluded them from approaching the police.

After this respite, it was back to 'ither auld drunk wives'. Margaret Haldane, a stout old Grassmarket beggar, once lodged at Log's with her disreputable daughter Mary. Mother and daughter shared a passion for the bottle, and left Log's before Burke and Hare's murderous career began.

Subsequently, however, Hare met old Peggy reeling drunkenly along the street, and invited her to come home with him. Burke joined them and drove away some children who were mobbing the old lady. At Log's, Mrs Haldane stumbled into the stable (or pigsty) to sleep off her liquor. Burke and Hare killed her there, noticing that she had but one large tooth in her mouth.

A cinder-gatherer named Effy also died in the stable. She sold Burke pieces of leather when he was up betimes about his business (a practice which earned him a favourable reputation for industry in West Port). Eventually she took up lodging at Log's, and Burke invited her back to the stable for whisky, where he covered her decorously with a cloth when she fell asleep. Then, with Hare's assistance, he murdered her.

Burke's good standing extended to the police. Constable Andrew Williamson found a drunken old woman sleeping on a doorstep, and was taking her off to the watch-house when Burke intervened, saying; 'Let the woman go to her lodgings.' Williamson replied that he didn't know where they were. Burke pretended that he did, took her back to Log's, and, thereafter, to Surgeon's Square. He made an interesting accidental confession when the *Evening Courant* pressed him about his familiarity with Williamson. He remarked that he had a good character with the police, for if they had known there were *four* murderers in the house they would have visited them often. It was the only time he let slip Laird and M'Dougal's full partnership in the gang.

By midsummer, Hare was boldly searching for victims (or 'shots', as he and Burke termed likely subjects) on the streets. He found a boozy old man who was persuaded to go with him for a drink, when an Irishwoman, accompanied by her deaf-mute grandson, overheard his accent and asked him for directions. To the old man's great disappointment, and good fortune, his promised drink evaporated, as Hare led his fellow-countrywoman and her charge back to Tanner's Close. Here, by Burke's account at the time, the old woman was suffocated in the back room while Mrs Hare (as Margaret Laird now called herself) kept the boy in front of the fire in one of the lodging rooms.

Burke confessed to simply suffocating him next, in the usual way. But Alexander Leighton, researching the case thirty years later, heard that in fact the murderers proposed to release the boy in Canongate, as he would be unable to communicate what had happened. But his growing distress worried them, and so Burke took him into the little room and snapped his spine across his knee. This vile brutality, Leighton believed, occasioned Burke's admitted sleeplessness, and his habit of going to bed with a candle left burning and a bottle of whisky to hand, from which to stupefy himself when guilty nightmares woke him up.

In any case, the two were packed into a pickled-herring barrel and loaded on to the horse and cart, which Hare had again acquired. The horse refused to proceed further than the Mealmarket, so they had to hire a porter to Surgeon's Square. The two bodies were only extracted with the utmost difficulty from their tight packaging (which might explain Knox's overlooking a broken back).

Soon after this horrible exploit, Burke and Helen M'Dougal went to visit her family near Falkirk. Mrs Hare suggested to Burke that he might take the opportunity to kill Helen and tell the neighbours she had stayed with her father. The Hares would have preferred to see the whole gang Irish. Burke refused, but may have agreed to substitute another member of Helen's family.

When the Burkes returned to Edinburgh, Hare was

surprisingly flush of cash. Burke asked him whether he had killed any more subjects in their absence. Hare denied it, but Burke found that this was untrue; he had killed and delivered an 'ither auld drunk wife'. Since the financial arrangements of the partnership always tilted in Hare's favour (he received an extra £1 from every fee as rental to Margaret, the landlady of Log's!) Burke strongly objected. He responded by leaving Log's, and taking lodgings in a tall tenement backing on a piece of waste ground a couple of blocks away to the east.

The new room was rented by a man called Brogan and his wife. It was the basement flat below the ground floor shop, and separated from the main West Portsburgh Road by a small cellar. Brogan's room was reached by steps down from the waste ground, which led into a fifteen foot long passage, at the end of which a door closed off a much shorter passage bending back to the right, and leading to the door of Brogan's room. The longer passage had other flats on either side. These single-room apartments were described as 'houses' in the Edinburgh dialect of the day.

This was sinister slumland, and a disquieting journey through unlit corridors at night. Most journalists gave spine-chilling accounts of Burke's squalid den and Hare's evil lair. So it is worth attending to the cool description Professor Wilson gave of them in *Blackwood's Magazine* following a daylight visit. Wilson's articles took the form of sprightly dialogues over dinner supposedly taking place between himself (as Christopher North), his maternal uncle (as Tim Tickler) and James Hogg, the great novelist and minor poet as himself (the Ettrick Shepherd).

> *Tickler*: Burke's room was one of the neatest and snuggest little places I ever saw – walls well plastered and washed – a good wood-floor – respectable fireplace – and light well-paned window. You reached the room by going along a comfortable, and by no means dark passage, about fifteen feet long – on each side of which was a room, inhabited, the one by Mrs Law, and the other by Mr and Mrs Connoway. Another short passage (with outer and inner door) turned off into the dwelling of Mr Burke – the only possible way of making it a room by itself – and the character of the

whole flat was that of comfort and cheerfulness to a degree seldom seen in the dwellings of the poor. Burke's room, therefore, so far from being remote or solitary, or adapted to murder, was in the very heart of life, and no more like a den than any other room in Edinburgh . . . .

Shepherd: But isna Hare's house a dreadfu' place? I howp it is, Sir?

North: It is at the bottom of a close – and I presume that one house must always be at the bottom of a close – but the flat above Hare's dwelling was inhabited, – and two of his apartments are large and roomy – well fitted for a range of chaff-beds, but not particularly so for murder. A small place, eight feet or ten by four or five, seems to have been formed by the staircase of another dwelling and the outer wall, and, no doubt, were murder committed there, it would seem a murderous place. But we have slept in such a place fifty times, without having been murdered – and a den, consisting of two large rooms, with excellent fireplaces and windows, and one small one, is not, to our apprehension, like a den of a fox or a wolf – nor yet of a lion or a tiger. The house outside looks like a minister's manse.

The separation did not entail splitting up the partnership. Instead, it provided a second venue for murder. Mrs Ostler, a porter's widow, came to wash for the Brogans. The laundry took her two days, and on the second, when Mrs Brogan had gone out, Hare came round with some whisky, which he and Burke shared with her. It made her sleepy, so they encouraged her to lie down and take a little nap. Soon she was boxed up in the coal-house off the passage, and during the afternoon she was sold to Dr Knox.

Next, Burke got even with Hare by carrying out a completely independent murder. Mary Haldane was becoming a memorable spectacle in Edinburgh. As late as 1860, people still remembered her crying through the streets in her tawdry finery, asking everyone if they had seen her mother. She dropped in on Burke at Brogan's one morning.

Every one else was out and Burke gave her some whisky. It left her sleepy, and Burke was delighted to see that she lay face downward on the bed. It made killing her easy, and he was able to box her up and deliver her to Surgeon's Square without the Brogans or Hare ever suspecting that she had visited him.

He was less successful with a young married cousin of Helen M'Dougal's former husband. Anne M'Dougal came on a visit from Falkirk. Though Burke may have engineered this in return for the Hares' promise not to harm Helen, he felt some compunction about eliminating his wife's family, and told Hare he would have to have most to do with her, as he did not like to begin the attack on a distant friend. So Hare stopped her breathing, and Burke confined himself to holding her down.

They lacked a box this time, but needed her out of sight before the Brogans returned home. David Paterson, Knox's dissecting-room porter, supplied them with a new trunk for the purpose, and during the afternoon they packed her up. But Brogan was suspicious on his return from work. He seems to have known there was a body in the trunk, and may have guessed whose it was. Burke and Hare, therefore, gave him £3, which was money he owed for the rent, and he absconded to Glasgow with it (and his wife), leaving Hare, as his cautioner, to settle up with the landlord. The £3 was never paid.

Burke and Helen now had Brogan's room to themselves. They decided to sub-let yet again. They took in Helen's first husband's married daughter, Ann M'Dougal Gray, with her husband James and their child.

The next and most notorious murder took place back at Log's lodging-house. 'Daft Jamie' Wilson was a well-known street character. A very sweet-natured idiot, he went about bare-headed and bare-footed because he thought times were too hard for him to accept the hats and shoes benevolent citizens tried to press on him. For the same reason he sometimes refused gifts of food.

He left home after his mother beat him severely for pulling down her china-cupboard and breaking all her crockery, but he saw her continually and took her his laundry. Jamie was scrupulously clean, changing his linen three times a week, and washing his slightly deformed feet daily.

He was a gentle youth of eighteen. Other boys – some as young as five or six – would challenge him to fight. Jamie stood trembling, with tears in his eyes, saying: 'Only bad boys fight.' When the little children finally hit out at him, he would laugh and run away, crying: 'That wasna sare! Ye canna catch me!' Everyone knew him by sight. Most people loved him.

Some time in October 1828 Margaret Hare found him in West Port looking for his mother. She told him she was at Log's Lodgings and led him back there. Hare gave him a drink, while his wife went out to Rymer's gin-shop at the top of Tanner's Close to fetch Burke.

Jamie was holding an empty cup, when Burke came into Log's, and Hare told him the drink was all gone. They sent Mrs Hare out for another mutchkin, and took Jamie into the little back room to wait for her. When she came back they sent her out. She locked the door from the outside, and pushed the key under it for them.

Jamie was not drunk but he lay on the bed, still wanting to know where his mother was. One of the assassins – each accused the other in this case – lay on him and covered his nose and mouth. Jamie struggled furiously, and hurled his assailant to the floor. With curses, the murderer called his companion to his aid. The three fought furiously. Jamie bit Burke in the leg, and the story went around that he had clenched his teeth in Burke's scrotum, giving him a wound that would prove mortal. It was untrue. The doctors confirmed later that Burke was already suffering from a cancerous testicle that would have killed him in due course.

The two men overcame their victim at length, and when his spasms had ended they stole his brass snuff-box and copper snuff-spoon.

Jamie's clothes were given to Constantine's almost naked children, who fought over them. Later a baker recognized a pair of trousers he had given Jamie on one of them.

Time was running out for the murderers by now. Abigail Simpson's daughter was volubly asking for her mother. Mary Haldane had been highly visible asking for hers. Mrs Lawrie,

Mrs Worthington and Janet Brown were whispering about Mary Paterson's disappearance. Daft Jamie's mother and sister were looking for him. Rumour hinted at a new gang of cannibals, like Sawney Bean's monstrous family who had once lived in a Scottish cave and eaten passing travellers. Sooner or later, questions must have led back to Log's Lodgings and Constantine's brother.

But before the public could trace them, Burke and Hare destroyed themselves by incautiously assuming that the Grays might prove as blind, deaf and bribeable as the Brogans or Constantine's family.

Madgy or Margery Campbell or Duffy or M'Gonagal or Docherty left her lodgings at Pleasance outside Edinburgh at dawn on 31 October to go and rejoin her son Michael who had recently moved into the city. Enquiring for him, she met Burke drinking in Rymer's at 9.00 a.m. Hearing her name and accent he promptly introduced himself, told her his mother had been a Docherty, and suggested that they might be relatives. She was easily persuaded to come back to his house, and was noticed by Mrs Law and Mrs Connoway – a tiny little woman, barely five foot tall, in a striking red gown and petticoat. Burke settled her with a drink and hurried out to tell Hare he had found a shot.

In the afternoon, Mrs Gray came home to find the little woman eating porridge, wrapped in her gown, and slightly drunk. Mrs Burke explained that they were doing her washing for her. Burke accused the Grays of quarrelling the previous night, and declared he would not have his house turned into a boxing-ring: they must leave immediately. Mrs Gray protested that she had been checking her child, but Burke was adamant. For the present they could no longer sleep in his room. Mrs Gray accordingly fetched out her family's clothes from the straw under the Burkes' bed where they slept.

When Gray came home from work, Burke accompanied them all over to Log's lodging-house, where they supped with the Hares.

While he was gone, old Mrs Docherty wandered into the Connoways' apartment, and let them persuade her that she was too tipsy to take herself out on the street. The Hares and

Helen M'Dougal came in with some whisky, and the women sang while Hare danced with Mrs Docherty and Helen M'Dougal. Mrs Gray glanced in while this was going on, having come back over from Tanner's Close to fetch a pair of stockings she had overlooked. She quickly concluded that the Burkes were having a private Hallowe'en party with their neighbours, and that was why she and her family had been so rudely bundled out.

The old lady hurt her foot in the dancing, and the Hares tried to persuade her to join them and Helen M'Dougal in a retreat to Burke's rooms. Mrs Docherty refused to budge until 'Docherty' (as she insisted Burke was called) returned. He arrived at 11.00 p.m. and took her with him.

Immediately a noise of fighting from Burke's room was heard by Mrs Law, Mrs Connoway and Mr Alston the grocer who lived in the flat above. The latter came downstairs to hear what was going on. As he reached the Connoways' door he heard a woman's voice screaming 'Murder!' After a few moments, he heard what sounded like a choking sigh, as though some one were being strangled. Then steps ran to Burke's inner passage; a hand slapped on the door sealing it off from the Connoways' passage, and the voice which had sighed cried: 'Help! Police! There is murder being done here!'

Mr Alston hurried out to the street to look for a policeman. The only one he saw was out of earshot, so he went back into the house. The fighting had stopped, and the screaming. There were men's voices talking quietly and peaceably. Mr Alston went to bed.

What had he heard? Initially, a fight between Burke and Hare. Burke asked Hare what he was doing when he found him in the room, and Hare instantly attacked his host. Mrs Docherty was distressed and tried to intervene, demanding that the other women come to 'Docherty's' aid. Thus far all accounts agreed. Burke, Hare and Margaret insisted that the fight was genuine, and certainly the murderers often fought each other when drunk. Some commentators, however, suspect that this scrap was fraudulent, its purpose being to 'accidentally' knock Mrs Docherty to the floor. This definitely happened, and according to Margaret Hare, the old lady then emitted the scream that attracted Alston's attention.

The others in the room all agreed that the screams and shouts came from Helen M'Dougal, who ran to the passage with Mrs Hare when the men either fought or set about the old lady. Both men interpreted these discreet withdrawals as proof that their womenfolk could not have been 'art and part' in the murders. Margaret Laird, under cross-examination, described their thoughts and conversation during this to-ing and fro-ing, and showed that life married to Burke or Hare was a constant hell of callous fear.

Q. Now, what more did you see?
A. I saw Burke lying on top of her, whether on her mouth or on her breast I could not say.
Q. Did she make a noise?
A. I could not say, for Mrs M'Dougal and me flew out of the house, and did not stop in it.
Q. You went into the passage, in short?
A. Yes.
Q. And you remained there some time?
A. Yes.
Q. Did you not cry out?
A. No, sir, I was quite powerless; and neither her nor me cried out.
Q. How long did you stay in the passage?
A. I could not exactly say, sir.
Q. A quarter of an hour?
A. I dare say it would be that, sir.
Q   Now, when you came back again, did you see the old woman?
A. No, sir.
Q. Seeing nothing of her, what did you suppose?
A. I had a supposition that she had been murdered. I have seen such tricks before . . . .
Q. What passed between you and [Mrs M'Dougal] when you were in the passage about a quarter of an hour? . . .
A. We was just speaking something concerning the woman; but I do not recollect what it was.
Q. Though you do not remember the words, you may remember the import of it?

119

A. Yes, sir . . . . We were just talking about her, saying,
    perhaps it would be the same case with her and I.

Q. (Court) Is that to say that you might be murdered; is
    that what you mean?

A. Yes, sir.

All this suggests that Burke's confession was true; that he
and Hare fought, occasioning some noisy upset from Helen
which Alston heard, and that the sigh or moan had nothing to
do with the suffocation of Margaret Docherty. She crawled
into the straw to sleep when the fight was over, while
Margaret and Helen got into bed above her. When Mrs
Docherty was asleep, Burke and Hare threw themselves upon
her, while the women slipped silently out into the passage and
whispered their fears for themselves. When it was all over,
and the body stowed in the straw, they came back in.

Burke hurried away to the nearby house of Knox's porter,
David Paterson, and met him coming home shortly after
midnight. Burke led him back to the murder room, pointed to
the straw under the bed, and said he had something fresh
there. Paterson told him to send it round in the morning, and
went home.

At 3.00 a.m. he woke up remembering another communication from a resurrectionist that evening. Merry Andrew had
sent a note to Surgeon's Square, reading:

> Doctor am in the east, and has been doin little busnis, am
> short of siller send out abot aught and twenty shilins way
> the carer the thing will be in abot 4 on Saturday morning its
> a shusa, hae the plase open.
>
> And. Merrilees.

Now this was that very season in which Syme was to cancel
his anatomy class for lack of bodies, and Syme had
approached Paterson to ask whether he had any surplus. The
coincidence that Andrew and Burke offered to deliver at the
same time meant that Paterson could come to a private
arrangement with Syme, and he went straight round to the
surgeon's house to say he was about to receive a body which
Syme could have for fifteen guineas. Syme was only too
pleased. But Andrew, having received his twenty shillings

Public dissection in Surgeons' Hall. The skeletons of famous criminals hang in the niches.

(*Above*) The dissecting-room in William Hunter's anatomy school, Great Windmill Street. Hunter presides in spectacles.

(*Left*) John Hunter. The father of comparative anatomy.

An impression of bodysnatchers at work by Dickens's illustrator, Phiz.

(*Top*) Watch tower in Berwickshire prefabricated from tombstones as a shelter for bereaved relatives guarding Lyemouth churchyard.

(*Above*) Young Robert Liston. Surgeon and bodysnatcher.

(*Left*) Dr Robert Knox, Burke and Hare's patron.

Burke in the dock.

Hare sketched in court, his nervous simper clearly visible.

Margaret Laird in court with Hare's baby.

Daft Jamie, Burke and Hare's most pathetic victim.

Helen McDougal pursued by the mob after her acquittal.

Sir Astley Cooper. President of the College of Surgeons and prominent patron of bodysnatching.

FOR THE GOOD OF POSTERITY.

I say Bill, have you heard of this march of Intellect? they say every Body will sell themselves.

A cartoon of 1829 commenting on the danger that intellectuals leaving their bodies to science might undercut the resurrection trade.

From Fairburn's transcript of the trial proceedings, 1831.

(*Top*) Cottage of Bishop and Head at Nova Scotia Gardens.

(*Left*) Carlo Ferrari with his cage of white mice.

(*Below left*) John Bishop.

(*Below centre*) Blaze-Eye Jack May.

(*Below right*) John Head.

advance, didn't show up, and sold his body to another buyer.

John Brogan, son of the former tenant, came to the tenement flat at 2.00 a.m. The Burkes still allowed him to frequent the place, and he saw them standing by the window, talking quietly, while the Hares were on the bed. Soon the women had given up the bed to the men and slept on the floor in front of the fireplace with Brogan. When he awoke, Burke and Hare had left, so he and the women moved into the bed together.

Burke now behaved with preposterous indiscretion. He invited the Grays, Mrs Connoway and Mrs Law to come and have a breakfast of whisky with him. And with the bottle only half empty, he sat on the bed and started throwing whisky on the ceiling and on to the straw under the bed, giving the absurd explanation that he wanted the bottle 'toom' (empty) so that he could get some more. Twice he sharply stopped Mrs Gray when she went to look in the straw for some more of her clothes.

When Mrs Gray asked where 'the old spaewife' was, Helen M'Dougal replied that Mrs Docherty had been 'owre friendly' with Burke, and she had 'kicked the drunken bitch's backside out of the house.' As the company broke up at the end of the morning, Burke told John Brogan to stay in the chair in front of the straw until he came back, while Helen M'Dougal stayed on the bed. Mrs Gray assumed that this was to keep her away from the straw which he had been disinfecting with whisky. She quietly got on with washing and sanding the floor, which occupied her much of the afternoon.

When Burke still hadn't returned by late afternoon, John Brogan and Helen M'Dougal deserted their posts. Mrs Gray went on cleaning up, helped by Mrs Law's maid, until her husband returned. Then she looked into the straw and found an arm. James Gray looked further, and uncovered the naked body of Helen Docherty with blood congealed around its mouth. The Grays gathered up their remaining property and hurried out of the place.

On the steps to the waste ground, Mr Gray met Helen M'Dougal. As he told it:

I asked what was that she had in the house; and she said what was it? and I said, 'I suppose you know very well what it is.' She fell on her knees . . . . In a supplicating attitude, imploring that I would not inform of what I had seen.

She went on to offer him five or six shillings to tide him over till Monday, and £10 a week for the remainder of his life if he would keep quiet. Gray flatly refused.

Helen went on into the dark passage and met Mrs Gray. Unaware that she had overheard the conversation, Helen repeated her offers to her. Mrs Gray repeated her husband's pious refusal, and asked her father's ex-wife what she meant by bringing the family into disgrace.

'My God,' cried M'Dougal, 'I cannot help it!'

'You surely can help it,' Mrs Gray replied sternly, 'or you would not stay in the house.'

The whole party debouched on to the street where they met Margaret Hare. She asked what was going on, and suggested that they go indoors to settle the matter quietly. They all went to a pub and wrangled for a little, after which Mr Gray went to report the matter to the police.

Burke's excellent reputation nearly saved him at this point. When it transpired that the Grays had been evicted the night before, the police concluded that this was all malice on their part. Nonetheless, Constable John Fisher was sent back to the tenement to calm everybody.

While the information was being laid, Burke and Hare had come back to the apartment with a tea-chest and a porter, and removed Mrs Docherty for instant sale to Dr Knox. On returning from this expedition, Burke was confronted by Fisher, who asked him where his former lodgers were.

'There's one of them,' replied Burke, pointing to Gray, and confirming that he had evicted him. Where was the little old lady? She had left at 7.00 p.m. the previous night, and no one had seen her since.

Fisher went into the apartment and saw blood stains on the bedding. Helen M'Dougal explained that a menstruating woman had slept there a week before, and they had not washed them since. By now Fisher was positive that the whole business was empty spite, but he asked one more question. When had Helen last seen Mrs Docherty? Helen replied that the old lady had left at 7.00 a.m. that morning to go to Pleasance, and she had seen her at the Vennel in the course of the day, when the old lady had apologized for her bad behaviour the previous night.

With this conflict in testimony, Fisher decided that the matter had better be thrashed out at the station. With the Burkes in custody, Mrs Docherty's clothes were found and identified. The Hares were arrested. The body was traced to Knox's the next day and identified. And the police waited for the surgeons' post-mortem to give them evidence of murder.

Dr Christison disappointed them. The state of the body was compatible with death by suffocation, but in spite of some bruising on the throat, there was no evidence that it had happened, and the old lady might have died naturally of a syncope while drunk. This honest report was a catastrophe for the authorities. It meant that there was not enough evidence to bring the gang to trial, and the whole of Edinburgh was seething with rumour and demanding further arrests and exemplary punishment.

Rumour ascribed up to thirty-two murders to the gang. Rumour asserted that Dr Knox knew very well that he was receiving murdered bodies, and asked the following pertinent questions:

(1) How could sixteen uninterred bodies be accepted without question as to their provenance?

(2) How came ignorant men like Burke and Hare to know a means of murder that left no signs of foul play?

(3) Was it true that Mary Paterson's body had been so fresh that the assistant receiving it was suspicious? That a student-client of hers had recognized her and said she was alive and well the previous night? And that Knox responded by having her hair cut off to disguise her, pickling her body for three months until she should be forgotten, and giving instructions that bodysnatchers were *never* to be questioned?

(4) Was it true that Daft Jamie had been recognized on

the dissecting table, but Knox had curtly denied it, nonetheless cutting off his head and identifiably deformed feet to give to his assistants for immediate research purposes?

There were clear answers to the first three questions. It is evident from Wight's arrest and Merry Andrew's career that there was a thriving trade in disinterred bodies brought in directly from the slums, and other surgeons' pretence that this was not the case was self-serving humbug intended to distance themselves from Knox.

Burke himself (later) confessed that suffocation had worked so well on Joseph the miller that he and Hare refined it for all future cases, without any instruction from anyone. Christison's examination of Docherty confirmed that suspicious-looking injuries to the spine might be the demonstrable result of tight packing after death.

Mary Paterson's body had, indeed, aroused doubts in assistant surgeon Henry Fergusson's mind, and he had asked when she died. Burke had complained that he would deliver no more bodies if he were to be catechized. But Knox had ordered Fergusson and the student who recognized her to question him again, and this time Burke admitted that she had been dead less than four hours on delivery, for she had died very suddenly in a drunken fit. He offered to take the doctors to the place where it had happened and produce witnesses. As the body stank of whisky, and Burke's manner was completely frank and open, the explanation was accepted.

Knox had also ordered Burke to cut off much of her long hair, as it contained curl papers which the anatomists did not want to waste time removing. She had been preserved in spirits for three months because she had an exceptionally beautiful physique, and Knox wished to save her for the part of his course that dealt with musculature, at which point he produced her as a perfect specimen. But, far from concealing her, he advised his students to draw her before she was cut up, as they might never again see so beautiful a specimen, and he invited in artist friends to sketch the cadaver before it was pickled. A surviving drawing proves that Mary did, indeed, have a remarkably lovely body.

The questions about Daft Jamie were never answered, but

in the light of the foregoing, it is safe to assume that there were innocent explanations.

The authorities held the gang throughout November. Burke's initial statement was absurd and obviously untrue. He described a complete stranger in a greatcoat and cape who brought a pair of shoes to be mended on Friday, and asked permission to leave a tea-chest by the bed while they were being done. Thereafter Burke discovered that the stranger had taken a body out of his tea-chest and hidden it in the straw under the bed. Burke protested and the man agreed to remove it. But he did not come back until Saturday at 6.00 p.m., when he brought a porter, and Burke accompanied them to Surgeon's Square, accepting two guineas from David Paterson as recompense for his warehousing. The body was not Mrs Docherty's : she was not nearly so tall.

This improbable tale became utterly ridiculous when Burke claimed that William Hare was the 'complete stranger' in the greatcoat!

His revised story was a great improvement. He accepted everything in the innocent witnesses' testimony down to the fight with Hare. After that, he said, Mrs Docherty crept into the straw to hide, and when they went to look for her, they found she had choked to death in her own vomit. So they decided to sell her to the surgeons.

As this was completely compatible with the medical evidence, a jury might find that, previous lies notwith-standing, there was 'reasonable doubt' whether murder had been committed. The authorities *had* to have a confession from one of the gang. The public would never stand for their being released.

Hare cracked in December. The authorities were careful to maintain that they had not offered him his freedom as King's Evidence if he confessed, and, moreover, by great good fortune it was Burke they particularly wished to see hanged if a choice had to be made. Both statements may be doubted, but the court and the press would have been unforgiving if the Lord-Advocate had admitted to negotiating Hare's freedom in return for Burke's conviction.

The trial of William Burke and Helen M'Dougal opened on Christmas Eve before Lord Justice-Clerk Boyle, supported by Lords Pitmilly, Meadowbank and MacKenzie.

Sir William Rae, the Lord-Advocate led for the prosecution. Sir James Moncrieff, Dean of the Faculty, led for Burke, and Henry Cockburn for M'Dougal. This star-studded team put on a magnificent display of legal argument.

The defence opened with an astounding attempt to prevent the libel (indictment) from being read, on the grounds that it was prejudicial to the prisoners and would be shown to be illegal. Cockburn and Moncrieff must have known that the court would never accept this argument to stop the trial before it started, but they also recognized that losing their first demand would win them a more sympathetic hearing when they presented their objections to the form of trial *after* the libel had been read.

Burke was indicted for the murders of Margaret Paterson, James Wilson and Marjory Docherty; M'Dougal as being 'art and part' to the third murder. Fifty-five witnesses, including Knox and his assistants, were to be called to prove these crimes.

The Dean of the Faculty promptly objected that felony had to be proved on the particular charge libelled. It was improper and unprecedented to enter three major crimes on one indictment with a promiscuous collection of witnesses to support them, and would prejudice the jury in considering each separate charge. The Lord-Advocate replied that felonies were often heard in groups, and pointed to cases of sheep-stealers who had been hanged for taking more than one sheep at one time. Moncrieff said that nobody had ever been charged with three murders at once. Rae riposted that nobody had ever *committed* so many murders as this gang! Both sides did their best to introduce precedents from the English courts, while insisting that they fully recognized they were not binding in Scotland.

Cockburn had a simpler task. He merely observed that it was wickedly prejudicial to M'Dougal to hold her in the dock while two murders in which she was not involved were tried. Rae's argument that it would be more prejudicial for her to stand trial after Burke might have been convicted of a murder was not very convincing.

The judges, mindful of the expense of repeated trials,

decided that the indictment should stand. But they told the Advocate-General that he could not present a mish-mash of witnesses and evidence, suggesting a wholesale atmosphere of continuous murder. He must present the evidence for one murder at a time. The order in which he picked the murders was up to him.

Rae behaved with utter propriety in choosing to open with Mrs Docherty's murder: the only one to which Helen M'Dougal was art and part. But everyone then and thereafter has lamented that in consequence we know all about the last 'drunk auld wife', and only sketchily about the most glamorous and the most pathetic of Burke's victims. Furthermore, Knox was not called in this case.

Mrs Docherty's movements from the time she left Pleasance to the time her body was discovered were established without much difficulty. Tension only arose when David Paterson tried to offer very self-serving evidence, suggesting that he had no idea that Burke would be offering him a body before it arrived, and that when it came he wanted nothing to do with it personally, suspecting that it had been strangled. In that case, the prosecution wanted to know, why had he sent his fifteen-year-old sister round to ask Burke to come and see him on the morning after Mrs Docherty died? Paterson was a very shifty witness.

But the real fireworks were reserved for the Hares, escaping the rope by offering King's Evidence. The defence team protested against possible deals behind the court's back. They objected to confederates testifying without corroboration. They were determined to prevent the prosecution from going on a fishing expedition to suggest that the murders libelled were only three among many that Hare knew about.

Yet they also demanded the right to attack Hare's credibility by asking him whether he had not himself been involved in many murders, both on and off the indictment against Burke.

The Lord-Advocate, on the other hand, had his own honour to protect. No matter what he thought of Hare, he had promised the man exemption from charges of murder, and he could not allow his witness to be self-convicted.

The court decided that Hare must be advised that he was

only required to testify on the murder of Mrs Docherty, and that he would not be prosecuted as long as he told the whole truth. Hare gave an unfortunate impression of flippancy when the Lord Justice-Clerk admonished him before he testified.

> Q. You will understand that you are called here as a witness regarding the death of an elderly woman, of the name of Campbell or M'Gonegal. You understand that it is only with regard to her that you are now to speak?
>
> A. T'ould woman, sir?
>
> Q. Yes.

Hare's question is understandable in view of Madgie Docherty's plethora of names and aliases. But it made a bad impression. So did his smirk and giggle.

His evidence was transparently false when he claimed that he sat on the bed for fifteen minutes, watching Burke kill 't'ould woman' single-handed. But it was damning proof that Burke was a murderer.

There was another legal wrangle when Cockburn's cross-examination moved to Hare's participation in previous murders. The Lord-Advocate insisted that it was irrelevant to the case; improper as an attempt to make Hare convict himself by his own testimony; and still more improper in that he had been ordered to restrict his evidence to Docherty's murder. Lord Meadowbank agreed. The other three judges accepted Cockburn's argument that it was always permissible for the defence to attack the credibility of a confederate witness for the prosecution, though in this case the witness should be reminded every time that he was not required to answer. Cockburn (though he protested) was satisfied with this judgment. Hare faced his damaging questions; accepted the warning that he need not answer; and damagingly chose not to answer.

Mrs Hare's testimony was punctuated by the yellow-faced baby on her arm. It had whooping-cough, and it screamed and whooped throughout her evidence. Cockburn felt that she deliberately distressed it when his cross-examination embarrassed her. Professor Wilson sourly noted that it was the image of Hare.

Mrs Hare did herself no good and Helen M'Dougal no harm. She confirmed that they were both out in the passage when the murders took place, and that they might themselves have been in fear for their lives. Moreover, it was she, not Helen, who had 'seen such tricks' before.

Cockburn achieved one more triumph in cross-examination, though it benefited Burke more than his client. He extracted from the doctors – especially Alexander Black the police surgeon – admissions that Mrs Docherty's appearance would have led them to conclude that she died of drink, had they not known the other circumstances. Cockburn's final speech excoriated the Hares.

It saved his client. After fifty minutes deliberation, the jury found the case against Helen M'Dougal Not Proven. Burke turned to her and said generously: 'You're well out of this trouble.' It was one of Cockburn's two greatest triumphs at the bar, and it enraged the general populace of Edinburgh.

Burke, inevitably, was found guilty. On Christmas Day, the judges gave Scotland the Christmas present it wanted: a death sentence for Burke. Their severities in passing sentence were merited. Nobody in Britain had ever murdered so many people, let alone for profit.

On Boxing Day, Helen was released. She made the mistake of returning to West Port, where the mob identified her, and only the police saved her from being lynched. Hare was held in gaol while Jamie Wilson's mother and sister made strenuous efforts to bring a private prosecution against him.

Burke's manner was generally contrite. He confessed to the authorities and the press, and expressed gratitude to the chaplains who visited him. But his sense of wrongdoing was perculiarly restricted. He felt aggrieved that Knox had only part-paid for Docherty's body, and wanted the balance made over to him, so that he might buy a presentable coat for his execution!

He was serious and penitent on 28 January when he walked out to the scaffold. But the furious execrations of the vast crowd visibly distressed him. He was hanged with a shockingly short drop, and struggled painfully for a considerable time. The mob yelled with delight, and the Edinburgh papers reproved their inhumanity.

The body was handed over to Professor Monro, and there was almost a riot when the mass of students were unable to get in to see it. Professor Christison checked that by arranging for the public to parade through and look at the muscular-thighed little corpse the following day.

There were violent demonstrations outside Knox's home in Newington and his dissecting rooms in Surgeon's Square. Knox was hanged in effigy and his windows were broken. 'Christopher North' made no secret of his belief that Knox had consciously bought murdered bodies.

His students, on the other hand, cheered him to the echo when he appeared at his lectures. And they were especially impressed when he calmly told them to ignore the mob howling outside, as it wanted his blood, not theirs.

The courts decided, regretfully, that the Wilsons's right to mount a private prosecution had effectively been waived once the Hares were accepted as King's Evidence. Hare was smuggled out of Edinburgh – indeed, out of Scotland – on 19 February, and was an unwelcome visitor at any coach stop where he was recognized. Eventually he made his way to the Midlands, where he was said to have found work at a lime kiln. In the end, his work-mates learned his identity and threw lime in his eyes, blinding him. He passed the last years of his life in London, probably in the fearful slums of St Giles, as several late Victorians remembered having the blind beggar in New Oxford Street and near the British Museum pointed out to them as Hare the murderer, when they were children.

The press ran stories highlighting the suspicious questions about Knox that had not been answered in the trial. David Paterson, who either left or was dismissed from his service, published a pamphlet seeking to exonerate himself by inculpating Knox. Press investigators learned of the body offered to Syme, however, and Paterson had to produce Merry Andrew's note to prove that he had not been so deeply implicated with Burke and Hare that he was actually ordering murders in advance, or bidding up the price of cadavers between surgeons before they had been delivered to him.

Knox kept a dignified silence until after the execution, and then arranged for a Committee of Inquiry to examine his role in the West Port murders. Its chairman was the Marquess of

Queensberry, but for reasons that were never explained, he resigned from it after a couple of weeks. The distinguished lawyers, doctors and scientists who remained published a report which criticized Knox quite sharply for the way in which he encouraged bodies to be received in his rooms without questions being asked. But they concluded, certainly correctly, that neither he nor any of his assistants had the faintest suspicion of foul play.

The populace was not satisfied. And the verb 'to burk', meaning either to kill in order to sell the body to anatomists, to kill secretly, or to suffocate, entered the language.

EIGHT

After Burke

Burke and Hare threw the surgeons into even more confusion than the Warrington cadaver-receiving conviction. Mass murder was not something that anyone could justify by its contribution to medical knowledge. The Edinburgh anatomists' first precautionary move was to join the populace in making a scapegoat of Knox. 'All ranks,' wrote St Robert Christison many years later, were persuaded that there:

> . . . had been blameable blindness and laxity on the part of Dr Knox in his transactions with these villains; and as for the mobocracy of the town, they looked upon him as "art and Part" with the active criminals, as he was their patron and encourager.

His colleagues might have acknowledged that mere chance had redirected Burke and Hare away from the incompetent Monro to the capable Knox. They did no such thing. They refused to serve on the committee of investigation under Lord Queensberry. They cold-shouldered the little one-eyed intellectual, and did their best to damn his memory.

Christison asked Knox how he could haved missed the abnormal freshness of warm and flexible bodies. And he pooh-poohed Knox's explanation that he believed the ten or eleven that had reached him in that state had been brought direct from the slums before they could be buried. Christison claimed that the long wakes held by the Scottish poor made such thefts far more difficult than they were in England. With characteristic humbug, he ascribed this special knowledge to information received from Professor Syme. (It would, indeed, have surprised Merry Andrew and Spune!)

Knox's students, on the other hand, passionately endorsed their teacher's rectitude and, to his extreme embarrassment, insisted on subscribing for a gold presentation cup as a testimonial of their esteem. It was in vain for Knox to plead that any memorial to the events of 1828–9 would always be inexpressibly painful to him. The cup was engraved and presented. Students continued to attend Knox's classes in greater numbers than his competitors', until the changed curriculum regulations of the 1830s forced them into the University's classes and brought all private anatomy academies into decline. The Edinburgh medical establishment maliciously pretended that Knox's falling fortunes were the well-deserved outcome of his personal failings. They impeded the careers of his loyal assistants and pupils. When he left Edinburgh for London in 1840, they put about the story that he was finally disgraced because he had proved himself a liar in a typical anatomists' dispute over priority of discovery of new facts. And Christison recorded his last days in an absolute travesty of the truth:

> [H]e sank, before his death in London, to a state not much above destitution. One of his last occupations was that of lecturer, demonstrator, or showman, to a travelling party of Ojibbeway Indians.

In fact, Knox entered general practice in Hackney, where he was noted for giving free obstetric treatment to the poor. His scientific curiosity directed itself to anthropology and he became a fellow of the London Ethnological Society and curator of its museum. It was under the respectable auspices of this learned society that he was involved with the touring Indians.

The medical profession closed ranks to present a respectable face to the public. On 8 January 1829 Edinburgh's anatomy teachers met with the Lord-Advocate 'with a view to an investigation being set on foot respecting the sources whence and the mode in which subjects have been recently supplied to our different Anatomical Schools.' The next day the Scottish Royal College of Physicians met, and a day later the College of Surgeons, both with a view to calming public apprehension, preventing future burking, and restoring the good name of the profession.

Did the Edinburgh surgeons also give up the practice of accompanying bodysnatchers to cemeteries for a little midnight adventure? It is impossible to be certain. But while their infamy was still fresh news, Mr Loftus of Newcastle renewed his investigations into suspicious packages transmitted via his coach office to accommodation addresses in Edinburgh. On 9 January it was reported that he had found the body of a three- or four-year-old child which might have been stabbed or strangled. It came off the York coach and might have been despatched from Wetherby. It would certainly have been sensible for the Scottish anatomists to buy imported cadavers for the time being.

York also provided the first detailed account of a new panic that occupied the public mind for the next few years: daylight pitch-plaster burking. Nobody was ever caught and charged with this crime, but there were many reports and rumours of attempts. The principle was simple. The burker seized his victim in a lonely spot, clapping a large plaster of soft thick tar and pitch over the mouth and nostrils. If this was done efficiently the victim would be promptly suffocated and prevented from crying out by the plaster while the burker had only to stop him from running away.

Three men in sailors' clothes tried this device on a York boy called Whitehead. They called at his mother's shop early in February 1829, and asked for lodgings. Mrs Whitehead had none to offer, and advised them to try a house in Paver's Lane. When they said they didn't know the way, she sent her little boy to direct them. In the quiet lane, they suddenly grabbed him and slapped their prepared plaster over his face. But (like all other pitch-plasterers recorded) they failed to cover his mouth completely. The disturbance attracted a girl to the stairs opposite and she shouted at them. The would-be burkers ran away, but were back in Walmsgate the next day, busking as distressed seamen. Young Whitehead saw them and raised a hue and cry. The men ran away along the Hull road, and were never heard of again.

It seems quite likely that the pitch-plaster was originally introduced as an aid to sexual assault. The earliest accounts spoke vaguely of 'the practice of attacking young females in the streets and attempting to fix plasters over their mouths for the purpose of frightening them.' Two or three inconclusive attacks were reported from Glasgow. Then in Nottingham a paedophile with a pitch-plaster was caught in the act by a mob and thought to be burking a child. They surrounded the place where he had decoyed a little girl and was assaulting her; rescued the child, and smashed the windows of a quack doctor they suspected of buying subjects for anatomy. The magistrates had to post a notice saying that the matter had nothing to do with burking.

Those who feared pitch-plasterers were advised to smear their faces with spermacetti, so that the plaster could not take a grip.

The extremity of panic was exemplified by a grazier who came to market in London during a heavy frost at the end of January. At night in his Smithfield lodgings he dreamed that he was being attacked by burkers. The nightmare so terrified him that he broke a hole in the ceiling and climbed out on to the freezing roof, where he shivered in his night-shirt and screamed 'Murder!', while rescuers had the greatest difficulty in reaching him across the ice-covered tiles.

For the first few months of 1829, missing people were automatically assumed to have been the victims of burkers: two children in Glasgow; a footman from St Paul's churchyard; an old woman named Bray who came from the country to visit friends in St Pancras; two elderly people who disappeared from Hackney.

With or without pitch-plasters, any form of mugging that entailed an attempt to muffle the victim led to thoughts of burking. A man in Birmingham was attacked at night by a gang in Moor Street who threw a sack over his head. His cries brought a constable to the rescue, and his fear that he was intended for the anatomists was not lightly dismissed.

The panic may have provided good excuses for persons

whose private lives meant that they needed to explain lost weekends to their families. Benjamin House disappeared in Coventry on Saturday 7 March. He reappeared the following Wednesday in Kenilworth with an elaborate tale of having been attacked by two men who bound and gagged him, and took him in a cart to a wood in Bedfordshire where it became apparent that they intended to murder him and sell his body to the anatomists. Happily a dog frightened them off, and he started to walk home, reaching Stony Stratford by Tuesday. As unlikely a story, on the face of it, as ever a guilty drunkard or fornicator put forward to cloak a few days' dissipation! But it passed muster at this season.

One improbable tale of attempted burking in the second week of February was vouched for by several Bow Street officers. A boy in south London had been sent out for his father's breakfast when he was stopped by a man near the Kent Road and asked to deliver a note to a certain house for a penny. The boy agreed, but took his father's breakfast home first. When he told his parents, the father recognized the address as a street with a bad reputation and insisted on looking at the note. Its melodramatic wording seems quite incredible: 'I send you another young subject – despatch!'

The father and some friends agreed to send the boy with the note and follow him closely. At the house he was led inside and the door shut immediately behind him. His father and friends forced their way in and found two men and a woman attempting to strangle the boy. The villains made their escape immediately, but two cadavers were discovered in the house. Kent Road was, of course, the neighbourhood of Crouch's retirement in the second half of the 1820s, and Blaze-Eye Jack May frequently lodged nearby. But *The Times* was obviously right to suggest that the story, as told, surpasses belief.

Nonetheless, bodysnatching was brisk in the south, as the press noted when reporting two corpses stolen from St Clement Danes' workhouse. But in Scotland, fear of burkers was so intense that an old woman took shelter with a respectable gentleman's housemaid, pleading that a resurrectionist had eyed her as they passed on the lonely road. When the master of the house came home it proved that he was the suspected 'burker', his sinister appearance caused solely by his being muffled up against the weather.

In Parliament, Henry Warburton realized that he could capitalize on public anxiety and push forward the work of his Committee. On 12 March he moved for permission to introduce a Bill to permit the legal custodians of a body to release it for dissection if they chose. He remarked that:

> he was happy in contemplating, that if his project was
> adopted, it would be the means of exonerating hereafter a
> beneficent and humane profession from the possibility of
> being implicated in the charge of being confederates with
> either resurrection-men, or a class of villains whose
> atrocities had so recently been brought to light.

And with no opposition, he was given leave to draft a Bill, which passed easily through its three Commons' readings in May.

There was a good deal of humbug and cant on both sides in the rather perfunctory debates. None of Warburton's opponents ever quite dared to say that they thought dissection reprehensible in principle. Nearly all paid lip-service to the need for continued research in anatomy, but there was much equivocation. Lord Tenterden asked: 'Why did Britain have so many anatomy schools when Paris got along perfectly well with two?' Mr Sadler said it was 'one of the most amiable feelings of human nature [that] induced the poor to prevent the bodies of their relatives from being dissected.' And Sir C. Forbes pondered: was there not a rule restricting hospital patients to one outside visit a week, so that 'a husband might enquire after his wife's health on one Tuesday and be told that she was getting well, and on the following Tuesday he might be told that she was dead and dissected?'

Warburton's supporters, on the other hand, were evasive in the face of the simple charge, put best by Lord Francis Osborne, who said he 'should decidedly oppose this measure, which gave over the bodies of the poor and friendless to the surgeon.' Peel was hauled in to summarize the better responses the anatomizers could make to this. The first was that the poor would benefit from having properly trained doctors and surgeons at all points in the profession. The rich could always pay extra for continentally trained doctors.

Less convincing was the suggestion that the poor would benefit more than the rich from the suppression of body-snatching, since more poor bodies than rich bodies were stolen. This was so obviously a consequence of the fact that there were more poor than rich to start with, that the anti-anatomists had little difficulty in turning the argument around and describing bodysnatching as a democratic pest that afflicted rich and poor alike, whereas hospital and workhouse delivery of the friendless was viciously class-biased legislation.

Still, the Bill went through, only to be suppressed by the Lords. The Earl of Malmesbury introduced it most half-heartedly, announcing that he was opposed to three out of four of its provisions. The Archbishop of Canterbury invoked the Principle of the Ripeness of Time, suggesting that further thought might mean that a less objectionable Bill could be presented in the next session. Their Lordships grasped eagerly at the Archbishop's lifebelt, unanimously concurring that 'something must be done' to help the anatomists and to suppress burking, but more thought was needed to make it effective.

For the next couple of years ordinary resurrectionists were liable to be taken for burkers. In 1831, a Yorkshireman called Pickering, who kept a school over the Rainbow Inn in Bond Street, Leeds, was arrested when, with two associates, he tried to place a large box addressed to Edinburgh on the courier coach for Carlisle. The box contained the dirty body of a man in his early twenties packed in sawdust. There were clear signs that it had been strangled.

Pickering kept a room in Tobacco Lane, Sheepscar, and when this was searched it was found to contain two earthy spades, a brace, a saw, a gimlet, rope, 'an instrument that might be used for breaking open coffin-lids' and a carpet bag holding wet and muddy fustian overalls. No great detective skill was required to identify the equipment of a grave-robber, yet the case was immediately reported as 'Supposed Burking at Leeds'. Only after the body was identified as that of a recent suicide, exhumed from Eardley, did the press shamefacedly reduce its accusation to resurrectionism.

The previous year, a valuable body in Walworth provoked bodysnatching competition. A young woman called Christy died of a complaint that the doctors could not diagnose. The Faculty was naturally anxious to recover her body and carry out a post-mortem. Several attempts to steal it before the funeral were frustrated by watchers. Then it was buried unusually deep at St John's Chapel. To no avail. A resurrectionist was stopped in Newington with the unfortunate Miss Christy's body in his sack. She was turned over to the coroner for a further inquest, where two men stepped forward as relatives, claiming the body for reinterment. Fortunately they were recognized as well-known resurrectionists, and the plot was frustrated. The coroner recommended that a watch be kept over her grave.

Two women, whose identity was never decisively established, recognized that the Walworth affair showed a means for frail females to enter the trade. When a man called Davis died in Dean Street, Soho, his body was claimed by a woman who purported to be his estranged wife. She moved it to her lodgings in Berwick Street, gave out that she was dissatisfied about the cause of death, and engaged a surgeon named Lane to carry out an autopsy for her. Oddly enough, he paid her £4 for the honour of making his professional services available. He and his assistant were arrested while transferring the body to dissecting rooms in Broad Street. The charges against them collapsed when they swore they had received the body from the next of kin and were returning it for burial after they had carried out the investigation required of them, and this was confirmed by 'Mrs Davis' and 'her daughter'. But the magistrates strongly doubted whether the two women were the people they represented themselves as being, and ordered that a close watch was to be kept on them if the parish returned the body to them for burial.

Probably the publicity given to the trade led to a considerable upsurge in part-time and free-lance bodysnatching. At the end of 1831, evidence emerged that gangs of bodysnatchers existed in Highgate, Bethnal Green and Whitechapel. But by that time burking had come to light in London.

NINE

The Bethnal Green Gang

National anxiety notwithstanding, it was more than two years after Burke's execution before anyone else was brought to justice for procuring anatomical specimens by murder. Then, at the end of 1831, the trial of John Bishop, James May and John Head, alias Thomas Williams, raised panic in London to hysterical levels.

In June 1830, Mrs Sarah Trueby let no.3 Nova Scotia Gardens to Mrs Sarah Bishop. The cottage was one of a row of three in a piecemeal development lying opposite The Birdcage public house on the borders of Bethnal Green and Shoreditch. The police allegedly described about two hundred dwellings meandering over the Gardens: contemporary large-scale maps show about twenty. Each cottage had its own 'garden' at the back, a little strip of land planted with occasional stunted trees and sooty gooseberry bushes and holding a privy at the far end from the house. Crude, knee-high paling fences separated the premises. It was over-populated and unlit, and to those accustomed to London's main roads, wild and lonely.

The garden of no.3 contained a large water-butt, sunk into the ground and covered by crude planks, which were themselves camouflaged with grass cuttings and leaf-mould. This doubtfully sanitary 'well' supplied water for all three cottages. The occupants of nos.1 and 2 had unrestricted access to it.

The row of cottages was owned by John Trueby, who lived in no.1 and let the other two. Mrs Bishop moved in with her husband, their three children and her sister-in-law (who was also her stepdaughter).

Thirteen years earlier Mrs Sarah Bishop had been the third wife of John Bishop's father, a Highgate carrier who, soon after their marriage, fell off the shafts of his cart and was run over by a Pickford's van. His widow inherited some of his property and continued to care for her infant stepdaughter, Rhoda.

Young John quickly secured the whole of his father's property and business by marrying Sarah six months after she had been widowed. He also became acquainted with a nest of criminal informers and professional (false) witnesses whose occupation seemed less demanding than loading and driving carts. They, in turn, put him in touch with resurrectionists who employed him to move a body from Holloway. After he had sold his business and squandered the proceeds, Bishop made bodysnatching his principal means of remuneration. He was well-known in 'the bodysnatching community' (probably the Spitalfields gang), but he also had a reputation for cowardice, refusing ever to participate in raids where resistance might be expected.

He preferred to disguise himself as a journeyman carpenter with a basket of tools, and lodge in any house where he heard that an occupant lay dead. Then, during his first night in his new rooms, he would sneak away with the body.

His timidity contrasted with his brutal, foul-mouthed, bullying manner, but matched his surprisingly sensitive appearance. His face was long, pale and thin, with lank dark hair that receded slightly at the temples as he approached his thirty-fourth year in 1831.

He claimed that newspaper reports of Burke and Hare's activities gave him the idea of commercial assassination. But he was probably encouraged by the new neighbour, who moved into no.2 Nova Scotia Gardens in July 1831.

John Head was another Highgate man who had fallen into criminal life. Born in 1805, Head was apprenticed to the building trade, and gave his occupation variously as a carpenter or bricklayer. In fact, he rapidly became a thief, and suffered repeated arrests for petty felonies. In 1825 he was lucky to have a seven-year sentence of transportation commuted. He then probably joined the Davis, Shearing and Knapp gang, giving the names Watkins and Williams on the two occasions when he was arrested with them. He gave Mrs Trueby his real name and the information that he wanted the building for his new trade as a tax-evading glass-blower. Thereafter he again passed himself off as Thomas Williams.

After six weeks or so he moved in with Bishop, increasing the crowded squalor of no.3, but giving the family the use of an empty house and garden for any felonious purpose.

Head was a rough-looking man, with something of a gaol-bird's hangdog slyness about him, but he was young and healthy enough to attract Bishop's sixteen-year-old half-sister Rhoda, and in September 1831 he married her. Bishop, as the papers noted with some bewilderment, was thus both his accomplice's father – and brother-in-law. In October, Mrs Trueby let no.2 to an older married couple named Woodcock.

Before the Woodcocks arrival, Bishop and Head had committed two murders, which they later confessed offici-ally. I believe that a young Bethnal Green woman with long dark hair also fell prey to them early in September, and that at least two other victims – possibly a black man and a boy – were also murdered before Bishop and Head saw Frances Pigburn sitting in a doorway in Shoreditch.

She was a 35-year-old unmarried mother who earned her living as a washerwoman. She lived with her sister, Mrs James Lowe of Chart Street, Shoreditch, but left home on the evening of Wednesday 5 October 1831 to go and lodge in Spitalfields. Mrs Lowe agreed to visit her there the following Monday. Possibly James Lowe objected to his sister-in-law, as Fanny made no attempt to return home when she and her little boy were thrown out on Friday night for having no money to pay the rent. Mrs Lowe went to Spitalfields three days later as arranged, and was astonished to learn that Fanny had not been seen all weekend.

Fanny and her son wandered up to the neighbourhood of Shoreditch church, where Bishop and Head found them sitting miserably on a doorstep. The two men expressed sympathy, and invited Fanny to join them for a drink. Late that night they were seen supporting her in the direction of Nova Scotia Gardens, where they put her and the child to sleep on a pile of dirty clothes.

Next morning they persuaded her to place the child with friends and meet them at the London Apprentice in Old Street Road at 10.00 p.m.

From 10.00 till 11.00 they had a sociable pint of porter apiece, and then Fanny was embarrassed at being seen by a gentleman who knew her – presumably she expected to pay for her night's lodging with sexual favours – so all three slipped out and walked away toward Bishop's home. They sheltered under a doorway from a rainstorm, went into The Feathers for another drink, finally returning to Head's empty house at no.2. No doubt the proposed sexual activity justified avoiding no.3 where Mrs Bishop and Mrs Head slept with the three Bishop children.

Bishop gave a quarter-pint of rum mixed with half a phial of laudanum to Fanny, who downed it in three gulps, after which she sat on the step leading into the wash-house at the back and passed peacefully into a doze. Bishop and Head were already feeling thirsty themselves, so they went back to the pub for another drink, and when they returned Fanny was unconscious.

They took off her plaid shawl and wrapped it over her head. They tied a rope to her feet and carried her out to the garden of no.3. And they lowered her head-first into the sunken water-butt.

The poor woman struggled very little as the cold water roused her. The top of the water bubbled a little. When all movement and bubbles ceased, the murderers tied the end of the rope firmly to one of the fence palings, and left their victim upside down in the water 'for the rum and laudanum to run out of her mouth', while they went for a walk to Shoreditch and back.

On their return they took the corpse back into no.2, leaving the shawl at the bottom of the well. They cut off Fanny's clothes, and threw them into the privy. They doubled up her body and stuffed it into a hair-box, which they corded up. And they left her to await collection while they walked over to Holborn for a porter.

Between four and five o'clock in the morning, Michael Shields was aroused by the burkers knocking at his door in Red Lion Square. He had worked as a porter ever since the Catholic chapel in Moorfields fired him from his post as watchman and caretaker for stealing silver spoons from the priests. As a watchman he had often worked actively with resurrectionists.

Shields went back with Bishop and Head to Nova Scotia Gardens where he insisted that one of the gang's wives must accompany him, carrying another piece of luggage as camouflage. Rhoda Head was given an empty hat-box, and after the gang had waited half an hour for the police to change watch, they set out for St Thomas's Hospital where Bishop expected to sell the body to J.F. South. At the Hospital, a footman confirmed that a body was wanted, but regretted that the surgeon was away until the next day, and no cadavers could be accepted until he had inspected them.

Bishop hurried from Lambeth to Southwark, where he offered his new subject to John Appleton, the porter at Grainger's. This time he made the sale, though Mr Dunn, the anatomist who examined the body, remarked that it was very fresh, and asked how it had died. He was satisfied on being told that it had been brought straight from the house where it died without ever being buried. And nobody but her family gave another thought to poor Fanny Pigburn for the next month.

The next murder to which the men confessed was that of a ten-year-old boy named Cunningham. Head found the child sleeping in the pig-market at Smithfield. He woke him up and persuaded him to come with them, and the two walked him back to Nova Scotia Gardens.

He was a little too young for the favoured potion of raw rum and laudanum. A gentler cocktail, diluting the opiate grog in warm beer and sugar, served to put him peacefully to sleep in one of Bishop's children's chairs, and his evil hosts promptly took him out to the well under cover of darkness, drowned him, and left him upside-down for half an hour. The next day he was sold to Mr Smith at St Bartholomew's Hospital for eight guineas.

The murder which led to the gang's arrest took place two days before Guy Fawkes Night. Head returned to Smithfield on the lookout for likely victims and he spotted a Lincolnshire drover's boy whom he had seen before. The lad was interested in his offer of a better job, and went with him and Bishop to Bethnal Green. They stopped on the way to buy him some soup and potatoes.

In Nova Scotia Gardens, the drover (whose age was variously estimated as between twelve and fifteen) was set to play with the Bishop children until dusk. He was given some bread and cheese and, long after dark, a full cup of rum with half a phial of laudanum in it. The boy swallowed this in two draughts, and accepted some beer as a chaser. In ten minutes or so, the two men forced their woozy victim into the yard, threw him to the ground, and lowered him headfirst into the well. It took about a minute for him to stop thrashing about and the bubbles to disperse from the top of the water. Then his feet were tied, the rope fastened to the paling, and he was left to drain for three-quarters of an hour while his murderers walked to Shoreditch.

On their return they pulled the body up by the rope, undressed it in the garden, rolled up the clothes and buried them on the spot. The body was carried into the wash-house and left for the night.

At ten o'clock the burkers arose and breakfasted with the family before going out together to The Fortune of War in Giltspur Street. Soon after mid-day 'Blaze-eye Jack' May came in to the tap-room. Both educationally and socially he was a cut above his coarse associates. Born near St George's Fields, he was the illegitimate son of a barrister and a laundress, whose strikingly good looks he had inherited. Young James was his mother's darling: she would scarcely let him out of her sight until he was twelve years old, and it was a mercy that she was no longer alive in this year of his public infamy. His father maintained a responsible interest in the lad, and had him educated at a boarding school, which taught him a good clerical hand. At the age of fourteen he was established as a law clerk in offices at 10 New Inn, where his father's chambers were. But this first foot on the ladder to respectable prosperity proved unexciting, and James was soon in trouble for idleness, insubordination and absenteeism.

When the exasperated law firm finally sacked May, he apprenticed himself successively to two Clare Market butchers. But that trade, too, prove more demanding than the lively scamp could tolerate, and he betook himself back to Lambeth where he set up a go-cart and spent his days taking passengers from the Elephant and Castle to Camberwell and Peckham and his nights transporting bodies for the resurrection men. When he crossed the river again, he took lodgings in Clare Market which enabled him to sack 'em up on his own account.

His rooms overlooked St Clement Danes's burial ground off Portugal Street. Soon May was slipping out at night and removing the body whenever he saw a funeral in the daytime. He boasted widely of the number of desecrations he had effected, and this had the unfortunate result of losing him all his respectable friends. In 1825, when he was arrested at Shoreditch, he was twenty-four. Henceforth his acquaintance was almost entirely criminal; his principal employment was bodysnatching. Yet all those who had known him previously agreed that he was a lively, humorous fellow, ready for any mischief, but absolutely untainted by cruelty. No one who knew him intimately could believe that he had any part in murdering a fellow-being.

Nor, in fact, had he. May showed himself, over the next day and a half, to be a far more professional tradesman in bodies than Bishop, as well as a more indiscreet, free-handed and incautious toper. But he had not seen Bishop for several months; had never met Head at all, and had unquestionably spent the entire night of the Lincolnshire cow-boy's assassination tucked up in bed with a good-natured prostitute. He had just left her arms when he came into the taproom at The Fortune of War.

Bishop immediately left Head drinking in the bar and went through to join May. He learned that 'Blaze-eye Jack' had been down in the country for a week, where he had acquired two excellent bodies that he had sold. May was flush with cash as a result, and ready to spend it. He stood Bishop a drink, and commented on the new smock-frock his friend was wearing, saying he wanted to buy one like it.

Bishop took him to Field Lane where May bought a smock-frock and put it on, which made the resurrectionists memorably identifiable. Nobody over the next twenty-four hours forgot if they saw a group of men including two (rather drunk) in smock-frocks.

When May insisted on buying drinks for a shopwoman, he began to embarrass Bishop, and the two returned to The Fortune of War where Bishop collected Head and took him away to the West End to arrange the sale of their body.

They went first to Windmill Street, where Bishop had recently promised Mr Tuson a subject. Mr Tuson told them angrily that he had been kept waiting so long that he had been forced to buy from another source the day before.

The resurrectionists went on to Dean Street, where Mr Carpue, after asking if the subject was fresh, offered them eight guineas.

Back in The Fortune of War the bodysnatchers, found May still in the taproom at 3.50 p.m. and still willing to buy them drinks. 'Blaze-eye Jack', however, was contemptuous of the price they had received and told Bishop he should have got ten guineas. Bishop agreed that if May could raise the price of the Lincolnshire boy he could keep all he fetched above nine.

The bodysnatchers had difficulty in getting a cab. A driver at the Old Bailey, whom they gave tea with gin in it, walked out on them when he learned their trade. Another at Black-friars Bridge refused to carry them. But walking back along Farringdon Road they spotted a bright yellow cabriolet, hailed it, and succeeded in engaging a driver at last. At 6.00 p.m. they drove to Nova Scotia Gardens where Head stood on the front wheel, smoking his pipe and chatting to the cabman while Bishop and May went in to collect the body.

As his first perquisite May took a bradawl, and brutally hacked out the boy's teeth, cutting his own hand in the process. He was in a hurry, and completed the extraction within ten minutes. The body was carried out in a sack by Bishop and May and loaded into the cab.

Mrs Channell of Virginia Road (which then ran con-tinuously from Shoreditch High Street to The Birdcage) watched suspiciously as her sinister neighbours hurried to conceal their load. Young Tom Trainer stood near her, and she told him to go and see what they were doing. The fourteen-year-old refused, fearing the ruffians would give him 'a topper' (a knock-down blow on the head).

The cab rattled away down Crabtree Row and made its way through the City and over the river to Guy's. John Davies, the head porter, greeted 'Jack' May cheerfully enough, but pointed out that he wanted no more subjects at present after the two he had bought from him the day before. So May and Bishop raced over to Webb Street to offer their body to Appleton at Grainger's. He too refused it, and with night coming on the men agreed to leave the body at Guy's and come back for it in the morning.

May gave firm and apparently self-incriminating instructions to Weeks, the Guy's under-porter. 'This thing is mine,' he told him. 'Don't let the subject go unless I am here with Bishop or I shall be done, for the body is mine.' Bishop did not contradict him.

After paying off the cab, the bodysnatchers went back to the Fortune of War. They invited its driver in for a further drink with them, and he remained in the bar with Head while Bishop and May went through to the tap, and Bishop made some ambiguous observations, which were overheard.

'What do you think of our new one?' he asked May. 'Don't you think he's a staunch one now? Didn't he go up to him well? I told you he was a staunch one. I told you it was all right, and if you stick to me, I'll stick to you.'

May said nothing as Head came in from the bar, and Bishop continued, 'There he comes. I told you he was a good 'un. 'Tis all right.'

'I don't know what you mean,' said May, which the police and prosecution took to mean that he knew very well Bishop was referring to the burking, but wanted to affect ignorance. But it may equally have been true that Bishop's incoherent commendation of his brother-in-law made little sense to May.

Next day Bishop and Head went back to Smithfield to greet Guy Fawkes's smiling morn with another drink at The Fortune of War. As they approached the pub, Bishop noticed a large hamper left behind the railings outside St Bartholomew's Hospital. This played a curious part in the case against the burkers. A Bart's porter was produced to testify that he had placed it there at dawn, but he was not asked why. Shields, whom Bishop and Head met in The Fortune of War, refused to fetch it, and Bishop had to go himself. But it was never suggested that the hamper had been stolen. Evidently the arrangement Naples had pioneered with Bart's had become regularized to the point that hampers were left out like empty milk bottles for any friendly bodysnatcher to collect.

With Shields carrying the hamper, the three then walked down to Southwark to meet May. He was again lodging south of the river, just off the New Kent Road, and he had spent a useful morning disposing of the teeth. He arrived at dentist Thomas Mills's premises in Newington Causeway shortly after 10.00 a.m. and sold him the almost perfect set for twelve shillings.

Mills washed the teeth and found little pieces of gum and membrane clinging to the roots. From this he deduced that they had been extracted quite soon after death, and the subject had, as May told him, never been buried.

May and Bishop, then, went to Webb Street to make one last attempt to sell the body to Grainger's. When this failed they went back over the river to King's College dissecting rooms between Lincoln's Inn Fields and Clare Market, where May asked porter William Hill whether he wanted anything.

'I don't care. What have you got?' Hill asked.

'A fresh male subject.'

'What size and what price?'

May told him the boy was about fourteen years old, and said he was worth twelve guineas. Hill doubtfully went to consult Mr Partridge, the anatomy demonstrator, who told him ten guineas was the maximum he might offer. Hill probably intended to cheat the hospital when he returned to the resurrection men and offered nine.

Bishop took the porter to one side, told him to ignore May who was drunk, and added: 'You shall have it for nine, and that within half an hour.' Hill learned that the subject was in the keeping of 'Williams' [Head], the third part owner, and Bishop quietly suggested that he should be told the price was actually eight guineas and the porter could keep half a crown of the extra guinea. Hill readily agreed, and later told the magistrates that such cheating was normal practice among bodysnatchers.

Bishop and May then left to fetch the subject, and returned some time after 2.00 in the afternoon with Head and Shields. May took the hamper from Shields and being quite drunk, threw the sack very roughly on the floor. Hill was surprised by the appearance of the body. The teeth had been extracted messily, leaving the lips badly swollen and lacerated and smearing blood over the neck and breast. The rib cage looked as though it had been broken (though this was probably the result of May's careless handling), and what struck Hill as quite extraordinary, the left arm was raised over the head and bent with the fist clenched. It had certainly never been in a coffin, and had evidently not received the last attentions of nursing or laying-out. Hill remarked that it was very fresh, and asked how it had died. May replied that he didn't know, and it was nothing to them as the subject *was* dead. Hill went doubtfully to Mr Partridge to arrange for payment, and some students came out to examine the new subject.

Like Hill, they were struck by its strange appearance, and some of them thought it matched the description of a boy who had been posted as missing. They hurried back to report their suspicions to Partridge, who came to see for himself. His practiced eye took in marks of violence to the back of the neck and he formed the instant opinion that this subject had not died naturally. Telling the bodysnatchers to wait while he fetched their money, he went to the college office and despatched porter Mayhew to summon the police. He also, ingeniously, collected a £50 note from the office.

Returning to the bodysnatchers he regretted that they would have to wait while he sent a porter to change the note. They objected strongly. Bishop demanded that Mr Partridge show them his own purse, and offered to take the four sovereigns there on account and return for the remainder on Monday. May offered to take the note himself and have it changed. Mr Partridge declined, and the wrangle was still going on when a body of constables from Bow Street arrived to arrest the gang.

They put up a furious resistance. May was particularly violent, and was trundled into Bow Street police station on all fours with his smock-frock over his head.

Superintendent Thomas took charge of the enquiry. What was Bishop's occupation, he enquired?

'A bloody bodysnatcher!'

And where had this particular body come from?

'Guy's Hospital.'

This was demonstrably misleading. The only male deaths in Guy's over the past week had both been adults in their thirties.

Hill told the magistrate how the body had aroused his suspicion, but was obviously shocked by the bench's ignorance of professional decorum when he was asked whether he had not thought to enquire where the subject came from.

'No!' he responded. 'We never ask that question!'

Magistrate Minshull remanded the men to Pentonville and Millbank prisons, and ordered that they should not be allowed to communicate with each other. And the police started preparing the case against them.

One look at no.3 Nova Scotia Gardens convinced Inspector Thomas that everybody knew what everybody else was doing in that tiny cottage with its two cramped living rooms at the front and minute wash-house at the back. He promptly arrested Sarah Bishop and Rhoda Head, and placed the children in the care of the parish.

PC Higgins was given command of the search parties. At May's lodgings he found a vice, a large gimlet, the blood-stained bradawl, and a pair of blood-stained corduroy breeches. In Nova Scotia Gardens he found more body-snatching equipment: spades and sacks, and a damaged chisel, which fitted the injury on the boy's neck. He also noticed a patch of freshly turned earth in the garden beside the well and dug up some boy's clothes: two blue jackets, one of them rather like a charity school uniform, and the other notable for its excellent cloth-covered buttons and finely finished buttonholes; two pairs of trousers, one very patched at the knees and fitted with dirty pink ribbon braces; and an extremely ragged shirt.

In the privy of no.3 the police found a woman's scalp with long dark hair, and some pieces of flesh. In the privy of no.2

they found Frances Pigburn's clothes. And a jumble of old clothes in Bishop's house included a ten-year-old boy's suit in excellent condition, and a fur cap with a green peak. Higgins's work was thorough, conscientious and useful.

Thomas was having a more difficult time, trying to establish the identities of the burkers' victims. A handbill describing the dead youth (4 foot 6 inches tall, well nourished with fair hair) evoked the suggestion that he might be one of the Italian immigrants who hawked statues of the saints in the streets. Enquiry elicited the fact that a boy named Carlo Ferrari, who used to carry a revolving squirrel cage containing two white mice and a tortoise, was missing. Various people who knew him – a Quaker stockbroker who gave him money near the Bank of England; Augustus Bruin who had brought him from Genoa and looked after him for his first three weeks in England; Mr and Mrs Pellagrini with whom he had lodged for several months – all came and inspected the body. Though Bruin burst into emotional French, crying: 'Ah, le pauvre garçon! Mon pauvre petit Carlo!' he, like the other witnesses, was unable to speak absolutely positively to his identity. The subject's mangled mouth and bruised face had altered his appearance substantially, and all that the witnesses could guarantee was the matching build, colouring and general appearance. The fur cap might have been Ferrari's, though there was conflicting testimony about its colour.

Enquiries in Nova Scotia Gardens were also unhelpful. The only witnesses purporting to have seen the boy in the neighbourhood were children, and the last-minute production of two adults, a labourer and a housewife, who also swore to seeing him with his cage of mice near The Birdcage, did little to help. It was rather too obvious that they had been coached to support evidence Bishop was disputing, and to identify the dubious fur cap.

The scalp in the privy proved equally disappointing. A woman who thought it might be her daughter's was positive that the clothes in the next-door privy were not, so that case went by default. But when Mrs Lowe identified Frances Pigburn's clothes, Thomas began to hope he had a strong secondary case. The Recorder of London told the Bow Street Magistrates' Office to take their time.

This was unfortunate for Mrs Bishop and Mrs Head. They flatly denied all knowledge of burking and bodysnatching, and the police were not going to find it easy to make a case against them. Mr Minshull directed that they should be released. But Thomas swiftly objected on the ground that they would return to Nova Scotia Gardens and destroy evidence. So the magistrates unwillingly allowed them to be remanded repeatedly until their husbands' trial.

At the inquest on the 'Italian boy' the bodysnatchers presented the defences they were to stick to throughout their trials. Shields was only the porter. May knew nothing about the subject's provenance, and only went along to help sell it for a commission. Head knew nothing about bodysnatching, and had only accompanied Bishop out of an overpowering wish to have a look at the building of King's College. Bishop, after an unsuccessful attempt to exploit May's injudicious claim that the body was his, fell back on claiming that he had obtained it by bribing two watchmen, and he nobly refused to name them as they had families to support.

May did not take kindly to Bishop's attempt to saddle him with obtaining the body, and attacked him violently in the police station as they were waiting to be returned to jail. Head's demeanour was consistently one of stolid unconcern.

Mr Woodcock and his son from no.2 Nova Scotia Gardens told of a great noise of quarrelling and fighting they had heard through the four-inch partition wall on the night of 3 November. It had ended when two men ran out into the garden, possibly chasing a third.

May used his final appearance at Bow Street to very good effect, eliminating the dim evidence of the blood-stained breeches in his lodgings, and exposing Thomas's excessive zeal to secure his conviction. When Higgins finished his testimony with the observation that the blood-stained bradawl in May's lodgings fitted the cut in his hand and the extraction marks in the boy's mouth and gums, May broke out:

> I admit all that; and what does it amount to? I did use the
> bradawl to extract the teeth from the boy, and that was in
> the regular way of business. And in so doing I wounded
> my hand very slightly. There is nothing very wonderful in
> that!

Mr Minshull warned the prisoner to consider whether what he said was doing him harm or good, but May went on, with aggrieved innocence: 'Now, Mr Policeman. You searched the house and say there was blood on the breeches. Do you remember the jackdaw in the place having hurt his leg with the door, and the leg bleeding; and that he afterwards sat upon my breeches?'

Higgins agreed that the landlady had told him this.

'You did not state that fact to the worthy Magistrate, which you ought to have done,' complained May.

Thomas leaped to his junior's defence. 'In justice,' he observed, 'I ought to say that when Higgins brought the breeches to me the blood appeared fresh and damp.' But Higgins honourably reminded him that he had carried them through a heavy shower of rain.

Shields's innocence was clear, and Mr Minshull dismissed him from the case, remanding him in custody until the Old Bailey trial in case the police wanted him as a witness. The other three were sent on for trial by jury, and Mr Minshull carefully warned them that there would be two counts in the indictment: of murdering Carlo Ferrari, and alternately of murdering an unknown boy. Bishop thanked him politely, although this tactic was a deliberate safety-net against the defence he was preparing which was intended to prove that the victim had been wrongly identified.

Bishop, Head and May came up before Mr Justice Vaughan in the Old Bailey on Friday 2 December. Charles Dickens, then aged nineteen, was in court making a shorthand report of the proceedings for an East End publisher. His description of the men expressed surprise that they did not look like stage villains.

> There was nothing in the aspect or manner of any of
> them which betokened a predisposition to anything like
> the outrage on humanity of which they stand convicted
> . . . . There was something of heaviness in the aspect of
> Bishop, but altogether his countenance was mild. Williams
> [Head] had that kind of aspect with which men associate
> the idea of sharpness and cunning, and something of
> mischief, but nothing of the villain. May, who was the

best-looking of the three, had a countenance which most persons would consider open and manly. There was an air of firmness and determination about him, but neither in him nor his companions was there the slightest physiognomical trait of a murderer, according to the common notions of the subject.

Twenty-eight years after the trial, Dickens created the fictional resurrection man, Jerry Cruncher, in *A Tale of Two Cities*. Three tiny echoes of the Bethnal Green burkers appear. Jerry (although not a burker) uses the curious simile 'as sleepy as laudanum'. He works over a coffin with 'some instrument like a great corkscrew'. And he refers insinuatingly to his merchandise as 'a Subject'.

Other observers agreed that the defendants did not look especially sinister. Bishop had retained his smock-frock, which gave him the air of a yokel with a street-smart face. May and Head in ordinary fustian looked respectively brutal and withdrawn, but by no means murderous. May's determined self-defence tended to outrage journalists lacking Dickens's perceptive precision.

The prosecution brought evidence of the defendants' arrest in possession of the body; of the fact that the boy had died violently, probably through the injury to his neck, which had broken a vertebra; of the bodysnatchers' peregrinations around London with their subject and its teeth; of the row Mr Woodcock had heard. The Italians made their rather less than positive identification of the victim; the children and the new witnesses claimed to have seen the boy near Nova Scotia Gardens on the day he died.

May had a perfectly good defence of alibi. Rosina Carpenter of Nag's Head Court, Golden Lane, swore that he had come to visit her between 4.00 and 5.00 p.m. on 3 November, and stayed until the following midday. Mary Ann Hall and Julia Lewis of May's lodgings at Dorset Street, New Kent Road, confirmed that his movements around that date supported her story. But all three admitted that they lived by prostitution, and this irrelevant fact rendered their pertinent evidence obnoxious.

Bishop was still less fortunate with his witnesses. He

subpoenaed Mrs Trueby and asked whether she remembered seeing some white mice in his garden.

'No, Mr Bishop, I never did,' the landlady replied.

'Did not your cat kill some of them?' Bishop pressed.

'No, sir. It never did.'

Mrs Dodswell, a clothes-seller of Hoxton, was equally unhelpful. Bishop put it to her that his wife had bought two caps from her a year previously, one of which was the possibly incriminating fur with the green peak. Mrs Dodswell adamantly swore that she had only sold Mrs Bishop one cap, and it was not the fur.

The judge took three hours to sum up the day's evidence. The jury took twenty minutes to find all three guilty, and at half-past eight Sir John Vaughan sentenced them to death, saying he concurred with the verdict which was supported by the most conclusive evidence.

'By false evidence, my Lord!' Bishop cried, and Head turned furiously on the Italian witnesses, who were in a little group near him, shouting that in a few months' time they would find themselves in a strange place as well as him.

May simply said: 'I am a murdered man, and that man [pointing at Bishop] knows it.' He remained quiet and dejected on his way to the condemned cell, as did Bishop. Head made an unconvincing show of carelessness. But it was he who cracked first, calling for Mr Wontner, the Governor of Newgate, and Mr Cotton, the chaplain, at 2.00 a.m., to whom he confessed that he had entrapped the Lincolnshire lad who bore such a surprising resemblance to the Italian boy, taken him with Bishop to Nova Scotia Gardens, and murdered him after dark. He added that May had nothing to do with the murder, and was brought in the following day to help dispose of the subject.

The trial had taken place on Friday. The execution was set for Monday. There were two days for the authorities to verify this confession, and respite May for eventual transportation. Bishop was showing signs of fear, and the Reverend Theodore Williams, Rector of Hendon, who had interested himself in the case, applied some extraordinary spiritual blackmail.

'Is there no hope for me of forgiveness from God?' Bishop asked him.

'I could not venture to give you an assurance of mercy,' replied Mr Williams. 'A man approaching the presence of his Maker with his hands stained with the blood of his fellow-creatures ought hardly to expect it.'

'Surely, Sir, there is a hope of mercy for a repentant sinner? Was not the thief on the cross pardoned?'

'Yes, but he had no knowledge of our Blessed Redeemer till that moment. But you have from your earliest days been taught to know Christ, and have rejected his precepts. Besides, yours cannot be called a true repentance – it is incomplete. Yours is more the fear of human punishment in consequence of the offence having been discovered than the repentance of a Christian. The first step toward a true repentance is a full and open confession of your crimes. Still, I exhort you to pray with all the sincerity and fervour you are capable of, and as the mercy of God is unbounded, your prayers may obtain favour in His sight.'

This sanctimonious bullying had its effect. Bishop admitted to trafficking in nearly 1,000 bodies during his career as a resurrection man. He thought that every resurrectionist in London had attempted burking since the Edinburgh trial gave them the idea. He confessed to the murders of the Lincolnshire boy, the boy Cunningham and Frances Pigburn, and exonerated May in a long statement dictated to Mr Williams. Head signed a confirmation that Bishop's statement was true. And Mr Williams raced with the papers to the sheriffs, who spent Sunday in applying for a stay of execution on May.

Yet Bishop's confession was transparently inaccurate. He claimed that Cunningham, like Pigburn, had been brought home very late at night, after the family had gone to bed, so that the family never saw them. He claimed that the Lincolnshire boy had reached Nova Scotia Gardens after dark, but before the family were abed, and so had been hidden in the privy for a couple of hours, with his bread and cheese and rum and laudanum smuggled out to him. This flatly contradicted Head's more probable and circumstantial story of finding the boys in the daytime, and bringing the Lincolnshire lad home to play with the Bishop children after a meal of potatoes and soup.

Bishop's motive, even in his state of spiritual torment, is

obvious. He wanted to protect his wife, sister and eldest son. There is no reason to doubt his and Head's agreement that their victim was not Carlo Ferrari, but a Lincolnshire drover who looked extraordinarily like him. Bishop's production of witnesses whom he cannot have expected to let him down, and the demeanour of both men on their conviction supports the view that they knew nothing about the Italian boy they have always been accused of murdering. The precise identity of the victim made no difference to their family or their fate; what mattered was that Bishop should pretend Sarah and Rhoda knew nothing about the dark doings in Bethnal Green.

And the same motive may have led him to suppress other murders. The press had turned up evidence of Bishop's making unsuccessful attempts to lure the young woman, originally identified as the owner of the scalp in the privy, to his house. We may assume that it was the gang's first effort, as no such mutilation was repeated; and that Mrs Bishop and Mrs Head were probably deeply implicated, since neither Bishop nor Head ever confessed to it or identified the undoubted remains. Yet on Sunday, rather to the satisfaction of pressmen who had found Mr William's holy inquisition a little distasteful, the burkers confessed to two other murders: another young boy and a negro. And Head added that he had forgotten two attempts that failed because the men had not succumbed to laudanum. By Monday both burkers apparently resented May's last minute reprieve, and were charging him with having tried and failed to dope two subjects.

The execution was a terrible occasion. The vast crowd broke down the barriers the police had fixed at the entries to Newgate Street, and two men and a woman were trampled to death. About thirty more people were seriously injured and sent to hospital.

May fell into a decline and died within a year on the hulks.

The case rang the death-knell of resurrectionism. This was burking moved to London. And before Bishop and Head were dead, yet another family had been charged with burking in the capital.

TEN

Eliza Ross

The last person to be executed for burking was already in custody when the Bethnal Green gang came to light. But initial difficulties in identifying Eliza Ross's victim, followed by a total failure to establish how she had disposed of the cadaver, meant that she was not brought to trial at the Old Bailey until Bishop and Head had been dead for a month, their naked bodies exposed to public view in the dissection rooms. Bishop had been exhibited appropriately in King's College, where students purloined locks of his hair as mementoes. His more muscular accomplice appeared in the Windmill Street Theatre, and the tattoo 'J Head' on his brawny left arm settled his identity finally.

Eliza Ross was also known as Eliza Cook after her common-law husband Edward. A fifty-year-old Londoner, Cook had been an Aldgate parish watchman before Peel's Bobbies replaced the incompetent old 'Charleys'. Redundancy then forced him into resurrectionism. His experience as a parochial officer taught him to remain silent under pressure, with a general deference to authority.

Eliza, on the other hand, a tall raw-boned Irishwoman of thirty-seven, had little control of her temper and let fly some of the most extravagant *obiter dicta* ever recorded from the dock. She was nominally a charwoman and huckster trading

159

in old clothes and animal skins at Rag Fair, the cheapest and most unsalubrious of the East End street markets.

Like many another skin-trader, she was suspected of kidnapping family pets for her wares. After her arrest, a broadsheet recorded an infamous exploit in Shadwell where she was said to have quarrelled with the landlady of the Sampson and Lion public house and taken her revenge by seizing the pub cat, breaking its neck, and skinning it on the spot with her bare hands. Unquestionably she was a local terror when primed with gin.

In 1829 she attempted the peculiar child-robbery that Dickens ascribed to 'Good Mrs Brown' in *Dombey and Son*. On a visit to Smithfield she saw a five-year-old boy named Harris in the street outside his father's jeweller's shop. She persuaded the child to accompany her through backstreets and concealed yards to Whitechapel and led him to Red Lion Court, where the Cooks lived at that time. There he became frightened, and a bystander stopped her from forcing him into her house. So she contented herself with stripping off his bib and tucker and taking a loaf of bread he was carrying, leaving the bystander to see the child home again.

In June 1831 a Goodman's Yard resident named Barry saw the Cooks and their little boy going furtively through the streets at 2.00 a.m. with a small sack. Knowing their reputation he had no doubt that it contained a child's body.

Early in August, Eliza was seen drinking in Southwark near Grainger's anatomy theatre with three resurrectionists. A couple of weeks later the Cooks prepared to leave Red Lion Court and move into Goodman's Yard.

They also urged their 84-year-old lodger, Mrs Caroline Walsh, to accompany them. She had lived next door to them with her granddaughter, Anne Buton, for six years, until Anne left in July for new lodgings in Playhouse Yard, Houndsditch. Instead of accompanying her, the old lady moved in with the Cooks. When they proposed moving to 7 Goodman's Yard she agreed to go with them. Anne tried earnestly to dissuade her grandmother.

'They'll cook you!' she said. 'They're bodysnatchers. They'll put a pitch-plaster over your mouth and sell your body at some of the hospitals.'

She gave the old lady strict instructions. She was not to leave Goodman's Yard that evening, and she was to wait in the following morning until Anne called round with stockings and household goods she wanted. Mrs Walsh agreed.

One hour after Anne parted from her, Mrs Walsh's other granddaughter, Mrs Lydia Basey, a boot-finisher's wife, came to Goodman's Yard to see how she had settled in. She spoke to her at the door, but did not go up to the attic room the Cooks had rented. Eliza's raucous voice floating down the stairs proved that she was in at the time.

At 9.00 a.m. on Saturday morning Mrs Buton came to 7 Goodman's Yard with her grandmother's stockings. Eliza was alone in the attic room washing a jacket and seemed confused as she explained that Mrs Walsh had gone out early intending to come back soon. Anne remarked that it was extraordinary for her grandmother to go out before 10.00 or 11.00 a.m., especially on this occasion when she had been asked to wait at home. Eliza's tangential reply was that Cook had liked the old lady and they had a jolly good supper the previous night.

'Glad you enjoyed yourselves,' said Mrs Buton stiffly. 'May I take the liberty of asking what was in it?'

Potatoes and meat, said Eliza, adding that Cook had gone out to fetch Mrs Walsh a drink of spirits. And a sack on the bed had been doubled up for her: 'We put her in it,' said Eliza incautiously, arousing all her visitor's worst fears.

To change the subject, Eliza drew attention to the jacket she was washing, and offered to wash anything of Mrs Buton's that she cared to bring. But she slipped again in remarking that she had not washed for Mrs Walsh, who was wearing no linen under her dress and petticoat. It was true, but Anne Buton wondered how Eliza knew?

Eliza responded obliquely with the story which was to be her defence from then on. She had gone out early in the morning for cinders, leaving Cook and Mrs Walsh contentedly smoking in chairs on either side of the fireplace. When she returned they had both left. And that was positively the last time she had seen Mrs Walsh. Now wouldn't Mrs Buton come out for a glass of gin with her while they waited for her grandmother?

In James Bishop's gin-shop at the corner of Goodman's Yard and the Minories, Eliza tried to probe her guest's suspicions.

'From what you say you seem to think we murdered the old woman.'

'I hope not.'

'From what you say, you think we destroyed her at our place.'

'Mrs Cook, you put the words in my mouth. What I suspect I don't say now. But you shall hear of it at length', said Mrs Buton darkly. She was to prove as good as her word.

The two women moved on to another pub, and Eliza, anxious to keep an eye on the suspicious granddaughter, tentatively invited her for lunch at the end of the morning. Mrs Buton agreed, and gave her threepence-ha'penny for bread and cheese. Then the two separated, Eliza to go back home, and Anne to search the neighbourhood for her grandmother.

For threequarters of an hour she traversed the streets of Whitechapel and Aldgate. Nobody had seen the familiar figure of the old hawker that morning. Eventually Anne gave up looking and went back to the pub to wait for Eliza and lunch. Here she waited two hours, before going over to Goodman's Yard to see what had become of her money.

She found Cook at home and in a savage temper. Eliza's face was severely bruised, and neither of the couple had much to say. When Cook went out, Eliza whispered that he had beaten her for going out with Anne, as he feared that she had let drop something she should not have done about Mrs Walsh. Mrs Buton said sympathetically that it was odd, as Cook looked so quiet.

'He's the greatest murderer in Europe, if the truth were known!' responded his common-law wife.

Anne Buton spent the afternoon making enquiries at jails and hospitals. They proved hopeless. In the evening the Cooks urged her to spend the night with them. Wisely, she refused, though a fine instinct for melodrama gave her an auditory hallucination on which to pin her suspicions. 'Nancy,' she claimed her Grandmother's voice came to her, 'what is the use of your looking for me when I have been suffocated in that bed of Cook's by him and his wife?'

Now she devoted the next two months to bringing the Cooks to justice. And this was no easy task for a poor working-class woman.

The police were not interested in following up her story, and Anne had to make her own enquiries first. As she gradually turned up evidence that Eliza Cook had offered some of her grandmother's things for sale she tried once more to interest the police in her complaint. Once more she was officially refused.

But Constable Lea, a local man, agreed to help her. His formal and official-seeming questions established that Eliza had offered at least eight women and one man in Rag Fair old clothes, rags, threads and tapes. She had added the suspicious request that they make no display of them but offer them furtively to selected customers. Most had therefore refused her. But three of them could describe or produce garments that definitely belonged to Mrs Walsh. Now there was enough evidence for a formal arrest for trading in stolen goods at the very least. Mrs Buton was triumphant as Officer Lea went to apprehend the family.

'God burn my soul in hell flames if I have done anything with her!' shouted Eliza on being asked about Mrs Walsh's disappearance. Lea stolidly took her and little Ned off to the cells, and went down to St Katharine's Dock where Cook was loafing with his cronies. He was much more amenable, as became a former constable, and simply said: 'Very well. It is proper that it should be enquired into.'

He arrived at the cells to find that enquiries had already begun. Starting with the weakest link, the police had questioned little Ned and received some half-hearted statements suggesting that his mother had burked the old lady. All three were locked up in separate but adjacent cells, through which the prisoners could communicate awkwardly by shouting from one to the next. Cook was in the middle, and the fascinated police noted down the following dialogue:

ELIZA Ned! Ask little Ned who told him to say what he has been saying about me?

COOK Ned! Your mother wants to know who told you to say what you have about her.

NED	Nobody.
COOK	Nobody.
ELIZA	Ask Ned how he came to say what he has.
COOK	How did you come to say it?
NED	Why, because she did it.
ELIZA	Oh! That we should have to suffer for what we know nothing about.
COOK	God knows that I had no hand in it. Never mind. There is nothing in this world that we should wish to live for. There will be forgiveness by God at the last moment.

This contrived and self-serving conversation prompted the police to fetch Henry and Caroline Mower, master and mistress of the National School at Aldgate, who successfully extracted a complete and damning statement from their unhappy little pupil.

At 10.00 a.m. on Friday 19 August the old lady had arrived at 7 Goodman's Yard with some bread. She went out for her day's work after eating, and returned at tea-time.

At 9.30 Eliza made coffee for the four of them to have with their supper, after which Ned and Mrs Walsh felt drowsy. Ned went and stood by the fire in the little eleven foot by thirteen foot room. Mrs Walsh lay down on the Cooks's large bed. Then, while Cook looked studiously out of the window, Eliza went over to the old lady, put her left hand firmly over her nose and mouth and held her down with her right hand on her chest. Mrs Walsh was too feeble to struggle, but Ned saw her eyes rolling desperately.

For nearly an hour this macabre tableau was held. Nobody spoke a word. Then Eliza picked up the body and took it away downstairs. Cook and Ned went peacefully to bed where the old lady had died, and the boy did not see his mother again until the next day.

In the morning little Ned was up at 7.00 a.m. for school. His parents had already arisen and gone out. As he was going to the privy in the yard, someone told him that there were some ducks in the cellar. This dark, rat-infested room was scarcely ever used. Ned decided to look for the ducks. He never found them. In the dark corner under the stairs he saw a bulging sack. Hanging out of its neck was Mrs Walsh's head, her streaked black and grey hair tumbled about her face, her eyes staring horribly.

At noon the boy came home for lunch to find his father beating his mother unmercifully for going out drinking with Mrs Walsh's granddaughter. Eliza was screaming and calling him a villainous murderer. Ned was used to such spectacles, and went out to play after his lunch.

That night his mother went downstairs after supper, and at half past ten Ned looked out of the window and saw her crossing the yard with a heavy sack. The following morning he heard her say to herself that she had taken the old woman's body to the London Hospital.

This detailed and circumstantial story was sufficient for the adult Cooks to be charged with murder. But their trial was delayed when the London Hospital doctors testified that their dissecting rooms had been closed for repairs during August, and no bodies were received. Their records did describe an old lady called Walsh who died. But they had listed her as Catherine, not Caroline, and she had reached them as a patient and not a cadaver for dissection.

The difference in the name was unimportant. Paupers were lucky to be listed under a misheard approximation of their real names. Mrs Walsh had come to the London Hospital from Hoxton Workhouse with a broken hip. She had died before recovering, and the authorities had buried her. Furthermore, as far as anyone could remember, she was not a tall old Irishwoman with well preserved teeth, but a mulatto.

The magistrates went to the trouble of having Mrs Walsh exhumed, and then disregarded Mrs Buton's testimony on 18 November that the broken-hipped mulatto's body was not her grandmother nor anything like her. They investigated the provenance of this body, and did not finally dismiss it from the case until the end of the month, when a laundry-mark on the shift in which it had been buried proved that it had indeed come from Hoxton Workhouse.

The search for Caroline Walsh's body went on until Christmastide, and the magistrates kept the case before them with repeated remands. Publicity given to Grainger's Academy led to enquiries there. Mr Appleton produced books to show that no body answering to Mrs Walsh's description had been received. In all probability a London Hospital porter accepted it on his own account, and sold it at a profit to another institution.

At the same time, Officer Lea had been sent to follow up Whitechapel's suspicion that the Cooks had murdered a fourteen-year-old maid-of-all-work named Sarah Vaizey, who had run away from her employers in Great Prescott Street, and was said to have taken shelter with the Cook family and never been seen again. Little Ned could not help in this enquiry. All he remembered was that a year or more earlier a girl had turned up looking for shelter. Eliza had told her they had no room, and the girl spent the night on the stairs.

Nor was Ned of any use in identifying the child's body supposedly being carried in a sack that summer. He simply denied ever having been up on the streets at 2.00 a.m. in his life.

At last, on 23 December, the magistrates sent Edward and Eliza on for trial, charged with the murder of Caroline Walsh and of a person unknown. The second charge, like the similar one attached to Bishop and Head's indictment, allowed for the possibility that Caroline Walsh might be shown to have had nothing to do with them, or for the Sarah Vaizey case to be brought if any further evidence turned up.

Eliza was stormily abusive on being committed for trial. 'It's too bad,' she shouted, 'to be thus treated for a dirty filthy old woman. She was all rags and tatters when I unfortunately took her into my room. Mrs Jones the landlady was quite shocked when she saw so ragged and wretched an old woman coming into her house, though some of the witnesses swore she was clean. But they would swear anything to be paid their expenses by the county. I am ashamed of such treatment in a country like England. My husband is an Englishman and fought for his country, and for him I am ashamed. But I hope I'll have a fair trial.'

The magistrates assured her that she would, and she calmed down, thanked them, and said she was glad she would not have to come to Lambeth Police Court again, as she feared being torn to pieces by the 'mob and gang' brought to the office by some of the witnesses.

Cook's patently false defence, taken in conjunction with Ned's statement, ought to have hanged him. He claimed that he and Eliza and little Ned had all slept together in the family bed, while old Mrs Walsh slept in her own bed in the corner. In the morning he had arisen early and gone out between 4.00 and 5.00 a.m. in search of work. On his return at about 8.30, Mrs Walsh had still been there, sweeping up the room before she went out to sell matches. That, he claimed, was the last he had seen of her. The adult Cooks' attempts to keep Mrs Walsh alive overnight and describe each other as the last to see her were transparently self-exculpatory lies. But Cook made a better impression than his wife because he did not explicitly accuse or even mention Eliza in the morning. Moreover he made an Uriah Heep-ish plea for little Ned's well-being, that, 'if we should suffer for this, that two or three gentlemen who I see here will take care of the boy and not let him want, though he has behaved so ungrateful, but I hope God will forgive him for what he has said.'

Eliza, by contrast, abused Ned whenever he appeared in court. She interrupted his first statement to the magistrates on 2 November by shouting: 'Good God! How could I have borne a son to hang me?' which made Ned cry and say how much he hated saying such things about his mother, but they were true. On his next appearance at Lambeth she shouted: 'Oh Ned! I hope you are not going to hang your mother!' and attacked him physically. The warders had to pull her off him. And when she finally faced her judges, she again hailed Ned's appearance as a witness with the sarcastic question: 'Have you come here to tell any more lies?'

But her worst fury was reserved for Anne Buton. She was a 'drunken, base strumpet!' She had given Eliza the damning clothes herself. She had given Ned money to testify against his mother – Eliza knew this, because she had seen him spending it in prison. In one of her softer moments (for Eliza was mercurial) she humbly thanked surgeon Jenkins of Great Prescott Street for coming forward to testify that he had never bought a body from her, and indeed, had never set eyes on her before coming into court. And after calling down God's blessing on him, she swung back on Anne Buton, crying: 'But as for you – you nasty drunken wretch – may the curse of God attend you – and you know you gave money to my poor boy to state what he has done – you wretch you have!'

By the time Edward and Eliza stood trial at the Old Bailey, interest was dying down. A relatively small crowd gathered at the court on 3 January, when the witnesses went through their testimony all over again, the Cooks protested their innocence once more, and the jury found Eliza guilty but, surprisingly, acquitted Edward. The court sent him back to prison to await any alternative charges.

On the scaffold Eliza still insisted raucously that she was innocent. Cook, too, denied Ned's story. The public was not entirely content that a woman should be hanged and her husband's life endangered on the testimony of their twelve-year-old son. (Ned's birthday had fallen over the Christmas recess.) So on 19 January Eliza's brother and Mr Harris, the jeweller whose son had almost been kidnapped by Eliza, arranged a confrontation between father and son in the workhouse where Ned was being cared for. The magistrates closely watched the two contradicting each other, and all observers came to the definite conclusion that Ned was telling the truth and his father lying. The magistrates ordered that Ned was to be placed in a charity school and his name changed so that he might not bear the stigma of having hanged his mother.

ELEVEN

The End of Bodysnatching

By the end of 1831, burkers and bodysnatchers were the most detested group in London. A woman in the Hackney Road was attacked by the mob for appearing in a shawl looking like one of the Bethnal Green gang's women. A Jewish clothes dealer in Field Lane, asked to give the police information about Bishop and May, refused the cab they sent for him as it was the sabbath. But he set out on foot, saying grimly that he would walk to Jerusalem to secure their conviction. And a tailor who had altered a coat for Head attempted suicide in his mortification at having worked for a burker.

Warburton was ready with a new Bill as London burking forced Parliament to set aside its Reform Bill squabbles momentarily and make time for legislation on anatomy. The Royal College of Surgeons had actually petitioned against his previous Bill, on the nit-picking grounds that Home Office licensing of dissecting academies would infringe their control of the profession, and the Murder Act of 1752 remained unrepealed. Warburton met these objections by proposing an inspectorate to report on the dissemination of cadavers, and suggesting a reversion to hanging in chains as a distinction marking that murder was more heinous than forgery or arson (in the royal dockyards). Fortunately, wiser counsels checked this last retrograde move towards the bloody code, and before

169

long forgers (though not naval arsonists) were freed from the threat of execution.

The radical 'Orator' Henry Hunt objected to the Bill on the old democratic ground that it subjected the friendless poor to posthumous mistreatment that the rich would not accept for themselves. He took up the earlier pamphleteer's suggestion that all surgeons should be compelled to leave their own bodies for dissection. But when it became clear that his campaign was foundering he allowed himself to become quite silly and threatened to introduce clauses forcing the dissection of all government job-holders (whom he deemed sinecurists). Despite vociferous pleading at every stage of the Bill's progress through the Commons, he achieved no greater amendment than a mean reduction in the salaries offered the inspectors.

Several people presented petitions against this legislation, some of which were obviously mischievous, like that of an atheist who claimed that he didn't care what happened to his body, but his Catholic wife did. Cobbett, too, came out in the open and petitioned Parliament against the Bill.

The debates on the subject were piffling. Nothing new was put forward. Despite encouragement from both sides, the devout Christians declined to state their known objection that whole bodies were required to rise at the Day of Judgement. Colonel Sibthorp, the voice of mindless John Bull reaction, suggested that legislative reform of anatomy was as unnecessary as the constitutional reform of Parliament, which was about to be passed. He was one of many who were also reduced to grumbling that these debates were very badly attended. By Parliamentary nonentities, he might have added. Peel, once again, lent Warburton's case weight rather than distinction.

The surgeons were murmurous that the Bill was permissive rather than compulsory. They wanted *every* body available, not just those that some authorities decided to release.

But they could not press the point too hard, given that Hunt's main point was true: they wanted the bodies of the poor since they couldn't coerce the rich. And anatomy's enemies were equally constrained by the undeniable fact that at least twenty bodysnatching murders had taken place over the last four years, and more might be expected if no action were taken.

In case anybody forgot the genuine alternative of the status quo, dissection and bodysnatching went their merry way, even as the new legislation wound its course through St Stephen's Palace. An Irishwoman demonstrated the terrible temptation anatomy held out to the destitute by offering her healthy two-week old baby to an apothecary as a subject for twenty-six shillings. A Hereford gang who had shipped bodies to London as hampers of poultry were arrested. William Davies made his last appearance in court on 12 March, in company with a newcomer aptly known as 'Boney' Dawkin. A wooden-legged pensioner was found with two friends slowly trundling a cart containing the bodies of two convicts, who had died on the hulks, along the New Cross Road on 13 April. A constable arrested them, and the bodies were re-buried at Plumstead. A week later Hollis was caught by the same constable in the same place with the same bodies. And with this final arrest he may be called the last of the resurrectionists.

Six weeks later the Lords approved Warburton's Bill with virtually no discussion. And bodysnatching was over.

The surgeons were not unfeeling towards those who had served them well. Murphy and Harnett had considerable savings, and the latter continued to deal in teeth from the Continent. Hollis had his horse and cart to earn his living. But Josh Naples was given humble employment at St Thomas's Hospital, which he retained until his love of the bottle led to his death. 'Patrick' (Wildes's) respectable working career was watched sympathetically by Bransby Cooper, and Tom Light's cab rattled through London without his former customers pointing an accusing finger at him.

A hospital porter called Tom Parker, who had been an occasional free-lance bodysnatcher (as well as the hangman who beheaded the Cato Street conspirators), reverted to his ancient skills in 1842 to show a young surgeon how to remove the head he wanted from a body in the London Hospital mortuary. (It required a sharp twist to one side before the knife slipped between the vertebrae.) And Parker then practised even more traditional skills in simulating the corpse's recapitation with sawdust and glue, and accusing the beadle of being drunk, when magistrates and a mob threatened to take violent action because the beadle objected that bodies in his care were being mutilated.

But the surgeons' final resentment was reserved for Warburton. His permissive legislation actually *reduced* the number of bodies available to them. The great dream of three to five bodies per student vanished for ever. The inspectorate ensured that no more illegally obtained cadavers could be smuggled in. Warburton was cursed as a timber merchant and no anatomist. His bill was excoriated as a feeble compromise, intended to satisfy the unscientific. The claim that it met the need for Christian burial was scoffed at with resolute acknowledgement that mangled remains constituting less than two-thirds of the original body-weight hardly made up a good audience for Gabriel's trumpet. The good old days of bodysnatching were regretted, when those extra guineas Ben Crouch demanded did at least ensure the supply of subjects. But always, always, the surgeons had to admit, *sotto voce*, that lamentable excesses had brought the trade to an inevitable end.

SOURCES

The Origins of Bodysnatching in England

Daily Universal Register, 21 Oct, 26 Nov, 27 Dec 1785
Edinburgh Evening Courant, 12, 19 Mar 1752
The Times, 20 Jan, 3, 21 Feb, 29 Mar, 24 Apr, 17 May 1786, 1 Jan 1787, 22
    Jan, 25 Nov, 29 Dec 1788, 31 Dec 1792, 23 Dec 1796, 9 Mar 1797, 10 Mar
    1798
Capt. L. Benson, *The Book of Remarkable Trials and Notorious
    Characters*, Chatto & Windus, London, n.d.
Zachary Cope, *William Cheselden*, E & S Livingstone, Edinburgh and
    London, 1953
Henry Fielding, *Examples of the Interposition of Providence in the
    Detection and Punishment of Murder*, A. Millar, London, 1752
Howard W. Haggard, *Devils, Drugs, and Doctors*, Harper & Bros, New
    York, 1929
John Kobler, *The Reluctant Surgeon*, Heinemann, London, 1960
George R. Mather, *Two Great Scotsmen: The Brothers William and John
    Hunter*, James Maclehose & Sons, Glasgow, 1893
C.H. Turner, *The Inhumanists*, Ouseley, London, 1932
Cecil Wall, *The History of the Surgeon's Company*, Hutchinson's,
    London 1937

The Origins of Bodysnatching in Scotland

Anon, *Groans from the Grave: or, A Melancholy Account of the New
    Resurrection, practised in and about Edinburgh*, Edinburgh, 1742
Robert Christison, *The Life of Sir Robert Christison, Bart., Edited by his
    sons*, Blackwood, Edinburgh and London, 1885
Alexander Leighton, *The Court of Cacus*, Houlston & Wright, London,
    1861
C.A.G. Mitchell, 'Anatomical and Resurrectionist Activities in Northern
    Scotland,' *Journal of the History of Medicine and Allied Sciences*, IV 4,
    1949
Robert Pitcairn, *Ancient Criminal Trials in Scotland*, Bannatyne Club,
    Edinburgh, 1833
Isobel Rae, *Knox the Anatomist*, Oliver & Boyd, London 1964

Helen Torrence and Jean Waldie

Caledonian Mercury, 14, 28 Jan, 4, 10 Feb, 19 Mar 1752
Edinburgh Evening Courant, 13, 27, 28 Jan, 4, 6, 10 Feb, 19 Mar 1752
Scots Magazine, Vol. 14, 1752
Scottish Record Office, Court of Justiciars Papers, Ref. JC 3/28

The Ben Crouch Gang

The Times, 27, 28 April 1801, 7 May 1802, 7 Oct 1803, 20 Apr, 15 Oct 1812, 10 Sep, 2 Nov 1813, 17 Feb 1814, 9 Nov 1816, 23 Jul 1819
Anon, *An Account of the Circumstances Attending the Imprisonment and Death of the Late William Millard*, Ann Millard, London, 1825
James Blake Bailey (ed), *The Diary of a Resurrectionist*, Swan Sonneschein, London, 1896
Bransby Blake Cooper, *The Life of Sir Astley Cooper, Bart*, Parker, London, 1843
C.L. Feltoe (ed), *Memorials of John Flint South*, John Murray, London, 1884

The Great Inflation

The Lancet, 25 Jan, 4 Dec, 1824
The Times, 15 Feb, 2, 9 Dec 1817, 3 Apr, 10 Aug, 17, 18 Dec 1818, 12 Jan, 22 Apr, 12 Jun, 7 Sep, 9 Oct 1819, 20 Feb 1820, 14, 15, 16, 22, 28 Nov 1822, 16 Jan, 21 Mar, 27 Sep, 15 Oct, 18 Dec 1823, 5 Jan, 4 Aug, 20 Oct 1824, 7, 31 Mar, 7 Apr 1825, 13 Jan, 16 Mar, 1, 26 Oct 1826, 1 Mar, 2, 24 Nov 1827, 31 May 1828, 12 Mar 1832
Anon, *An Account of the Circumstances Attending the Imprisonment and Death of the Late William Millard*
Bailey, *The Diary of a Resurrectionist*
Charles Brook, *Battling Surgeon*, Strickland Press, Glasgow, 1945
Bransby Blake Cooper, *The Life of Sir Astley Cooper*
Pierce Egan, *Boxiana, Vol.IV*, Sherwood, Jones & Co, London, 1824
Henry Downes Miles, *Pugilistica Vol. II*, Weldon & Co, London, 1880
Reports from Committees of Parliament No. 568, *Select Committe on Anatomy*, HMSO, 1828

The Golden Age in Scotland

The Lancet, passim, 1826
The Times, 26 Dec 1811
Christison, *The Life of Sir Robert Christison*
Alexander Leighton, *The Court of Cacus*

Henry Lonsdale, *A Sketch of the Life and Writings of Robert Knox the Anatomist*, Macmillan, London 1870
– *The Anatomical Memoirs of John Goodsir*, Adam & Chas. Black, Edinburgh, 1868
C.A.G. Michell, 'Anatomical and Resurrectionist Activities in Northern Scotland'
William Roughead, *Notable British Trials: Burke and Hare*, William Hodge, Edinburgh, 1948

Burke and Hare

Anon, *A Correct Account of the Life, Confession, and Execution of Willm. Burke*, G. Caldwell, Paisley, 1828
Christison, *The Life of Sir Robert Christison*
Henry Cockburn, *Memorials of His Time*, Fontes, Edinburgh, 1909
Alexander Leighton, *The Court of Cacus*
Henry Lonsdale, *A Sketch of the Life and Writings of Robert Knox the Anatomist*
R.H. Nimmo, *Wretch's Illustrations of Shakespeare*, Nimmo, Edinburgh, 1832
– *Noxiana*, Nimmo, Edinburgh, 1832
Isobel Rae, *Knox the Anatomist*
William Roughead, *Notable British Trials: Burke and Hare*
John Wilson, 'Noctes Ambrosianae XIX', *Blackwood's Magazine*, Edinburgh, March 1829

After Burke

Caledonian Mercury, 8, 14 Jan 1829
Morning Advertiser, 19 Nov 1831
Morning Post, 14 Nov 1831
The Times 8, 16, 27 Jan, 2, 3, 9, 10 Feb, 11, 21 Mar 1829, 9, 17 Apr 1830, 10 Feb, 21 Mar, 27 May 1831
Christison, *The Life of Sir Robert Christison*
Hansard, *Parliamentary Proceedings*, 1829
Henry Lonsdale, *A Sketch of the Life and Writings of Robert Knox the Anatomist*
William Roughead, *Notable British Trials: Burke and Hare*
John Wilson, 'Noctes Ambrosianae XIX'

The Bethnal Green Gang

Morning Advertiser 9, 10, 14, 22, 24, 25, 26, 28, 29 Nov, 3, 5, 6 Dec 1831
Morning Post, 7, 19, 21, 23, 24, 25, 26, 28, 29 Nov, 2, 6 Dec 1831
The Times, 7, 19, 21, 22, 24, 25 Nov, 3, 5, 6, 9, 12, 13, 16, 24, 29 Dec 1831

175

Charles Dickens [supposed ed. and transcriber], *Burking the Italian Boy!
Fairburn's Edition of the Trial of John Bishop, Thomas Williams, and
James May*, Fairburn, London, 1832
Martin Fido, *Murder Guide to London*, Grafton, 1987

Eliza Ross

Morning Post, 6 Dec 1831
The Times, 28 Oct, 3, 4, 17, 18, 25, 29 Nov, 5, 23 Dec 1831, 7, 19 Jan 1832
Martin Fido, *Murder Guide to London*

The End of Bodysnatching

British Medical Journal, Vol 295, July 1987
Morning Post, 22, 26 Nov 1831
The Times 24 Nov, 2, 5, 6, 13 Dec 1831, 10, 23, 28 Jan, 2, 4, Feb, 12 Mar, 19
Apr 1832
Hansard, *Parliamentary Proceedings*, 1831–2
C.L. Feltoe (ed.), *Memorials of John Flint South*
William Roberts, *Mr Warburton' Anatomy Bill, Thoughts on its
Mischievous Tendency; with suggestions for an entirely new one founded
upon an available anti-septic process*, J. Ollivier, London, 1843

INDEX
=====

NB   con   =   constable
         por   =   porter
         res   =   resurrectionist
         stu   =   student
         s/a   =   surgeon/anatomist

A Tale of Two Cities, 44
Aberdeen, 20
   Medico-Chirurgical Society, 19
Aberhethy, John, s/a, 13, 50, 81
Acts of Parliament
   Anatomy Act 1832, 64, 65, 169–70
   Murder Act 1752, 8, 88, 169
   Reform Act 1832, 169, 170, 171
Aldgate, 75, 159, 162, 164
Aldwych, 32
Alston, Hugh, grocer, 118, 120
Anatomical Club, 38, 52, 54
Anderson, Andrew, stu, 25, 27, 28
Appleton, John, por, 144, 148, 165–6
Arthur, James, stu, 21, 22, 23–4, 25, 28
Artichoke Tavern, 59
Ashton, Thomas, res, 80
Atkins, George, undertaker, 43
Austin, Charley, res, 60

Bailey, James Blake, author, 44
Baillie, Matthew, s/a, 9, 13
Barclay, John, s/a, 16, 89, 90, 91, 97
Barry, ···, Goodman's Yard resident,
   160
Basey, Lydia, d. to Caroline Walsh, 161
Batten, ···(?Hutton), con, 74
Beckenham, 61
Bedall, Joseph, res, 70
Bedfordshire, 136
Bedminster, 80
'Beggar's Hotel, The', 105
Bell, Sir Charles, s/a, 33, 97
Bentham, Jeremy, 69
Berlin, 15

Bermondsey, 74, 75
Bethnal Green, 71, 140, 158
Bethnal Green gang, the, 71, 139,
   140-158, 159, 169
Binnie, Sir Ralph, JP, 70
Birdcage, The, public house, 140, 147, 152
Birmingham, 135
Bishop, James's gin-shop, 162
Bishop, John, res, 71, 72, 140-58
Bishop, John sr, 141
Bishop, Rhoda, d. to John *see* Rhoda
   Head
Bishop, Sarah (Mrs John Bishop), 140,
   151, 153, 156, 158
Bishop of London, 77
Blackfriars Bridge, 147
Blackman Street, 12
Blackwood's Magazine, 109, 113–14
Blenheim Steps Dissecting Academy,
   33–4, 38, 82
Blundell, William, stu, 80-1
Bow Street magistrates' office, 64, 79,
   136, 150, 152, 153
Box, Richard, res, 80
Boyle, Lord Justice-Clerk, 125-7
Bray, Mrs, suspected burkers' victim, 135
Bridgman, Edward Little's Patent Iron
   Coffins, 76–78
Bristol, 80
British Museum, 130
Brodie, Sir Benjamin, s/a, 33, 81
Brogan, John jr, Burke's lodger, 121
Brogan, Mr and Mrs John, Burke's
   landlords, 113, 114–15, 117
Brookes, Joshua, s/a, 33–4, 38, 47, 62, 81–2

Brown, H.K. ('Phiz'), 94
Brown, Janet, prostitute, 109–11
Brownrigg, Mrs Elizabeth, murderess, 9
Bruin, Augustus, immigrant, 152
Bruntsfield Links, 92
Bryant, Mr, postmaster, 55
Bunhill Row burial ground, 52
Burke, Constantine, b. to William, 104,
   109, 110, 111, 116, 117
Burke, Elizabeth (Mrs Constantine
   Burke), 109–10, 111
Burke, Mrs William, 105
Burke, second Mrs William, *see* Helen
   M'Dougal
Burke, William, 103, 104–31, 132
burking, supposed, with pitch-plasters,
   134–5, 160
Butler, Daniel, res, 35–7, 41–2, 44, 46, 48,
   50, 52, 54, 55, 58, 67
Buton, Anne, d. to Caroline Walsh,
   160–3, 166
Butter, Margaret, Edinburgh housewife,
   28
Buzzard, Mr, churchwarden, 77–8
Byrne, Charles, 'the Irish giant', 7

C ·· ··, Mr, secret anatomist, 32, 36
Cameron, David, carter, 101
Campbell, Madgy or Margery, *see*
   Docherty
'Canbery Bess' Evans, murderess, 9
Canongate, Edinburgh, 103, 109, 112
Canterbury, Archbishop of, 138
Capper, Mr, JP, 51
'Captain, the', Irish GP, 99
Carlisle, 138
Carpenter, Rosina, prostitute, 155
Carpue, Joseph, s/a, 34, 38, 62, 147
Cato Street conspirators, 82, 171
Cave, ·· ··, res, 72
Caversham, 72
Channel, Mrs, of Virginia Road, 147–8
Chapman gang, the, 40, 48–9, 56, 62, 85
Chapman, Israel, body-stealer, 40, 48,
   49, 52, 62, 85
Chart Street, 142
Cheapside, 4
Chelmsford, 79
Cheselden, William, s/a, 3–5
Cheshire, 108
Christison, Sir Robert, s/a, 56, 90–1,
   95, 102, 123, 124, 130, 132
Christy, Miss (decd), 139
Clare Market, 146, 149
Clare, Revd Mr, 77
Clarke, Samuel, res, 79

Clerkenwell, 43, 71, 74
Clift, William, s/a, 32
Cline, Henry, s/a, 13, 32, 35, 65
Coach and Gate Inn, Gracechurch
   Street, 36
Cobbett, William, 63, 68, 170
Cochran, ·· ··, carter, 18
Cochburn, Henry (Lord Cockburn),
   104, 126, 128, 129
Coldbath Fields Prison, 67
Coles, Thomas, res, 70
Colewort, Hants, 78
Company of Barber-Surgeons
   (Edinburgh), 14
Company of Barber-Surgeons
   (London), 3, 4, 14
Company of Surgeons, 5
Connaway, Mr and Mrs, Burke's
   neighbours, 113, 117, 118, 121
Cook, Edward jr, s. to below, 160, 164–8
Cook, Edward sr, former con, 159–68
Cook, Eliza *see* Eliza Ross
Cooper, Astley, s/a, 4, 13, 32, 35, 36, 40,
   41, 54, 57, 58, 59, 62, 63, 64, 65,
   68–9, 70, 76, 79, 81–2
   account books of, 60, 63, 65
Cooper, Bransby, s/a, 4, 40–2, 44, 45, 50,
   55, 58, 60, 61, 62, 63, 66, 68–9, 79, 171
Cooper, Lady, w. to Astley, 68
Cotton, Revd R.H.S., 156
Couchman, ·· ··, por, 64–5
'Country Tom' Sherwood, murderer, 9
Court of Justiciars, Edinburgh, 28
Coventry, 136
Cowgate, Edinburgh, 27
Cowper, William, s/a, 3
Crabtree Row, 148
Crawford's Burial Ground, 59
Cribb, Tom, prizefighter, 75
Crouch, Ben, res, 37–41, 42, 44, 45, 46, 47,
   48, 49, 50, 52, 54–7, 58–9, 60, 62, 63,
   65, 66, 67, 73, 83–5, 86, 87, 90–1, 92–4,
   136, 172
Crouch gang, the, 37–55, 62, 70, 72
Crouch, James, res, 60, 61, 62
Crouch, Sarah (decd),, 60
Cruikshank, William, s/a, 9, 13, 16, 33
Cullen, James, s/a, 91–2
Cullen, William, physician, 16
Culzean, Mikey, doss-house owner, 105
Cunningham, ·· ··, murder victim, 144, 157
Cures, 93
'cutting', 39–40, 47, 52–4, 65

Dalkeith, 22, 23
Dallas, Charles, s. to below, 23, 27

Dallas, Janet Johnston, w. to below, 22, 23, 24, 25–8
Dallas, John, chairman, 22, 24, 25, 26–7, 28, 30
Dallas, John jr, s. to above, 22, 24, 25, 27, 28, 29–30
Davies, William, res, 70, 71, 74, 81, 86, 171
Davis, John, por, 148
Davis, John, stu, 80–1
Davis, Mrs and Miss, body-stealers, 139
Dawkin, 'Boney', res, 171
Dean Street Anatomy Theatre, 38, 139, 147
Desmond, ···, pensioner, 197
Dickens, Charles, 94, 154–5, 160
Dickson, 'Half-hangit Maggie', 18
Docherty, Margery, murder victim, 117–23, 124, 125, 127, 128, 129
Dodswell, Mrs, clothes dealer, 156
Dombey and Son, 160
Donaldson, Esther, res, 10
Doncaster, 37
Donegal militia, 104–5
Dorset Street, Kent Road, 155
Drummore, L.J., 29
Dublin, 12, 81, 99
Duffin, Thomas, res, 73–4
Duffy, Margery *see* Docherty
Duitt, William, rapist, 9
Duke of York's Hospital, Chelsea, 34
Duncan, George, stu/res, 92
Dyott Street, 10

Earl's Court, 7
Edinburgh, 12, 17, 66, 78, 81, 91, 96, 97, 99, 100, 101, 105, 108, 112, 123, 138, 157
    Academy, 96
    Evening Courant, 107, 108, 111
    Infirmary, 90
    University, 15–16, 17, 18–19, 89, 90, 91, 96, 98, 103, 133
Effy ···, cinder-gatherer, 111
Egan, Pierce, 37, 75–6
Elchies, L.J., 29
Ellis, ···, sometime Bow Street Runner, 64
England, 32, 99
Europe, continent of, 41–2, 56, 85
Ewer Street, 59
Excellent, HMS, 42
Exeter 'Change menagerie, 33

Fair, John, h. to Jean Waldie, 23–4, 27
Fairclough, Jane (decd), 80
Fairlie's Close, 22, 23, 25, 31

Falkirk, 112, 115
Farringdon Road, 147
Feathers, The, public house, 143
Ferguson, Henry, stu, 92
Fergusson, Henry, s/a, 124
Ferrari, Carlo, street-entertainer, 152, 154, 158
Field Lane, 147, 169
Fisher, John, con, 122–3
Fisherow, Edinburgh, 18
Fleet Ditch, 70
Flint, James, stu, 21, 22, 23, 25, 28
Forbes, Sir Charles, MP, 137
Forth, River, 92, 93
Fortunes of War, public house, 145, 146, 147, 148
Frampton, ···, s/a, 44
France, 41
Fraser, Nellie, alewife, 22, 24
Freemasons' Tavern, 38

Genoa, 152
Gibb's Close, Edinburgh, 109–10
Gilbert Gow's wineshop, 24, 27
Gilbert, Mr, widower, 77–8
Gilbert, Mrs (decd), 77–8
Gill, Dr William, 78
Gilmerton, 96, 108
Giltspur Street, 145
Glasgow, 15, 105, 115, 135
    University, 16, 19
Glennon, James, con, 53, 81, 86
Golden Lane, 155
Goodman's yard, 160, 161, 162, 164
Gordon, William, res, 15
Goswell Road, 76
Grainger's Anatomy Academy, 62, 63, 67, 82, 144, 149, 160, 165–6
Grainger, Edward, s/a, 62, 63, 67
Grainger, Richard, s/a, 63, 66, 67
Grassmarket, Edinburgh, 30, 105, 111
Gray, Mr and Mrs James, Burke's lodgers, 115, 117, 121–2
Gray's Inn Lane, 77
Great Marlborough Street, 33, 82
Great Prescott Street, 166, 167
Great Windmill Street, 8, 9, 50, 147
Great Windmill Street Dissecting Academy, 8, 11, 13, 33, 34, 40, 62, 159
Green, ···, s/a, 66–7
Green Man Inn, Barnet, 55
Greyfriars churchyard, Edinburgh, 17
Griffin, ···, con, 51–2
Guildhall, 12
Guy's Hospital, 10, 35, 37, 40, 148, 151

Hackney, 133, 135
Hackney Road, 169
Haddon, ··· , res, 18
Haggerston, 79
Haldane, Margaret, murder victim, 111
Haldane, d. to above, 111, 114–15, 116
Hall, Edward, res, 80
Hall, Jack, res, 74
Hall, Mary Ann, prostitute, 155
Hamilton, William, stu, 11–12
Hampstead and Highgate Horse Patrol
    (Bow Street runners), 49
Hare, Mrs William *see* Laird
Hare, William, 103, 104–31, 132
Harnett, Jack, res, 12, 42, 44, 48, 49, 50,
    52, 58, 60, 171
Harnett, William, res, 12, 36, 40–1, 44, 48,
    49, 50, 52, 58, 60, 171
Harper, ··· , cemetery keeper, 46, 48, 72
Harris, ··· , jeweller, 160, 168
Harris, ··· , s. of above, 160, 168
Harris, George, res, 59, 61
Haymarket, 50
Head, John, res, 71, 72, 140–58, 159, 169
Head, Rhoda, *née* Bishop, 144, 151, 153,
    158
Henderson, John, res, 78
Hendricks, ··· , res, 32
Hereford, 171
Hickman, Tom 'the Gasman',
    prizefighter, 75–6
Higgins, Pc, 151, 152, 153, 154
Highgate, 71, 139
Hill Cliff Baptist churchyard,
    Warrington, 80
Hill, John. gravedigger, 59, 72
Hill, William, por, 149–51
Hogan, Hames, murderer, 9
Hogg, James, 'the Ettrick Shepherd', 109,
    113–14
Holborn, 10, 50, 52, 73, 79, 144
Holborn Hill, 74
Hollis gang, the 60, 61, 63–4, 81
Hollis, William, res, 44–6, 47, 48, 49, 50,
    59, 60, 61, 63, 69, 74, 86, 171
Holmes, John, res, 10
Home, Alexander, Advocate Deputy, 29
Hornig, ··· , s/a, 44
Hornsey, 75
Horse Wynd, Edinburgh, 27
Houndsditch, 160
House, Benjamin, lost weekender, 136
Howard, 'Praying', res, 101, 103
Hoxton, 47, 156
Hoxton workhouse, 165
Hunt, Henry 'Orator', MP, 170

Hunter, John, s/a, 6–7, 9, 10, 13, 16, 32, 35
Hunter, William, s/a, 5–6, 7–8, 11, 13, 15,
    16, 82
Hunterian Collection, 5, 7
Hutton, ··· , con, *see also* Batten,
    Sutton, 50

Inverask, 18
Ireland, 32, 99,

Jerron, John, res, 72
John, Archduke of Austria, 55
Johnson, John, res, 78–9
Johnston, Janet *see* Janet Johnston
    Dallas
Joseph, ··· , miller, 107–8

Kay, Miss, cemetery owner, 45–6
Kelly, Thomas, res, 70
Kenilworth, 136
Kensal Green, 74
Kent Road, 70, 136
Kenyon, J.L., 11
King, ··· (decd), 70–1
King's College, Aberdeen, 15
King's College Hospital, London, 149,
    159
King's College, London, 63, 153
Kingsgate Street, 10
Kinmuck, 20
Knapp, William, res, 70, 71–2
Knox, Mary, sis. to Robert, 97
Knox, Mrs, midwife, 30
Knox, Mrs Robert, 97
Knox, Robert, s/a, 91, 96–9, 100, 103, 107,
    108, 114, 122, 123–4, 126, 127, 129,
    130–1, 132–3

Laird, Margaret (Mrs William Hare), 106,
    108, 110, 111, 112, 116, 118, 119–20,
    122, 127, 128–9
Lambert, ··· , con, 48, 51
Lambeth, 50, 59, 60, 70, 73, 166
Lancet, The, 4, 63, 68, 69
Lansdowne, Margaret, suspected res, 71
Law, Mrs Janet, Burke's neighbour, 113,
    117, 121
Lawrie, Mrs, probable procuress, 109,
    110, 111, 116
Lea, Pc James, 163, 166
Leeds, 78, 138
Leighton, Alexander, journalist, 102, 112
Lewis, Julia, prostitute, 155
Leyden, 15, 16
Libberton's Wynd, Edinburgh, 28
Libertoun, 18

Light, Tom, res, 44, 48, 49, 50, 51–2, 171
Limekilns, Scotland, 92
Lincoln's Inn Fields, 6, 149
Lincolnshire boy, murder victim, 145–51, 157, 158
Liston, Robert (Sir), s/a and res, 16, 57, 89–94. 97, 98
Little Leigh, 70
Liverpool, 78, 99
Lizars, John and William, s/as, 97
Loftus, Mr, coach proprietor, 78, 99, 134
Log's Lodgings, 106, 107, 108, 111, 113, 114, 115, 116, 117
Logue, ···, doss-house keeper, 106
London, 8, 15, 32, 34, 64, 72, 78–9, 81, 82, 84, 133, 135, 158, 169
London Apprentice, pub, 143
London, City of, 148, 157
London Ethnological Society, 133
London Hospital, 10, 33, 40, 48, 67, 68, 84, 165, 166, 171
Long, ···, res, 71
Lonsdale, Henry, s/a, 91, 94, 98, 103
Lowe, Mr and Mrs James, n.o.k. to Frances Pigburn, 142, 152
Ludwig, Archduke of Austria, 55
Lynn, R.v., 10–11, 80

M'Dougal, ···, adulterer, 105
M'Dougal, Anne, sis. to Helen, 115
M'Dougal, Helen (Mrs William Burke), 105, 110, 111, 112, 115, 118, 119, 120, 121, 122, 123, 125–7, 129
M'Gonagal, Margery *see* Docherty
M'Nab, Sandie, ballad-singer, 91–2
MacKenzie L.J., 126–7
Maidstone, 61
Maidstone Prison, 51
Malmesbury, Earl of, 138
Mansion House, 36
Marden, George, res, 65
Margate, 56, 84
Marr, James (decd), 19
Marshall's Disssecting Academy, 10, 12
Marshall, William, res, 73–4
Marshall, William, s/a, 10, 12, 13, 33
Mason, Mr, night-stroller, 51
Matthews, ···, groom (decd), 72,
May, James 'Blaze-Eye Jack', res, 72, 136, 140, 145–58, 169
Meadowbank, L.J., 126–7
Mealmarket, Edinburgh, 122
Merrilees, 'Merry Andrew', res, 100–3, 120–1, 124, 133
Merrilees, Sarah (decd), 101
Methodists, 45, 100

Middlesex Sessions, 49, 70
Miles, H.D., boxing historian, 37
Millard, Mrs, w. of below, 66–7
Millard, William, por/res, 52, 65–7, 76
Millbank Prison, 151
Miller, Thomas, advocate, 29
Mills, Thomas, dentist, 149
Mills, Thomas, res, 71
Minshull, Mr, JP, 151, 153, 154
Minto, L.J., 29
Mitchell, Margaret *see* Mary Paterson
Moncrieff, Sir James, advocate, 126
Monro, Alexander I, s/a, 15, 17
Monro, Alexander II, s/a, 15
Monro, Alexander III, s/a, 15–16, 90, 91, 96, 97, 103, 132
Monteith, Alexander, s/a, 14
Moor Street, Birmingham, 135
Moorfields, 144
mortsafes, 20
Mounsey, Dr Messenger, 9
Mount Pleasant Burial Ground, 46, 60
Mowatt, 'Moudiewarp', res, 100, 101, 103
Mower, Mr and Mrs Henry, schoolteachers, 164
Muiravonside, 105
Murphy gang, the, 58–9, 60, 61, 65, 75, 85–6
Murphy, ?Patrick, res, 52, 58, 59, 60–1, 63, 64–7, 69, 73, 74, 76, 79, 84, 85–7, 171
Musselburgh, 17, 18, 22, 23

Nag's Head Court, 155
Naples, Josh, res, 42–4, 48–51, 52, 58, 59, 60, 65, 81, 84, 87, 95, 102, 149, 171
diary of, 43–50, 56, 58, 74, 84, 85, 87
Neat, Bill, prizefighter, 75
Nether Keith, 17
New Cross Road, 171
New Inn, 145
New Kent Road, 149, 155
Newcastle, 78, 134
Newgate Prison, 5, 156
Newgate Street, 158
Newington Causeway, 149
Newington churchyard, London, 12, 51
Newington, Edinburgh, 130
Newington, London, 139
Newman, Mr, coach operator, 55
New Oxford Street, 130
Nicholls, Frank, s/a, 6
North Berwick, 17
North, Christopher *see* John Wilson
Northolt, 70, 71
Nottingham, 135

Nova Scotia Gardens, 140–1, 143, 144, 145, 147, 151, 152, 153, 157

Ojibeway Amerindians, 133
Old Bailey, 5, 147, 154, 159, 168
Old Street Road, 143
O'Neill, Mrs (decd), 99
Orrey, 104
Osborne, Lord Francis, MP, 137
Ostler, Mrs, laundress, 114
Oxford Street, 33

Palmer, Mr, barrister, 80
Paris, 6, 15, 96
Parker, 'Lousy Jack', res, 12, 41
Parker, Tom, res, 171–2
Parliament, 76, 88, 137–8, 169
 (*see also* Acts of; *and* Select
  Committee)
Partridge, Richard, s/a, 149, 150
Paterson, David, por, 103, 115, 120–1, 125, 127, 130
Paterson, Mary, prostitute, 109–11, 117, 120, 123, 124, 126, 130
'Patrick' ·· ·· , res *see* Wildes
Paver's Lane, York, 134
Peebles, 106
Peel, Sir Robert, 55, 137–8, 159, 170
Pellagrini, Mr and Mrs, Ferrari's
  landlords, 152
Peninsular War, 41–2
Pentonville, 71
Pentonville Prison, 151
Penycuik, 96, 101, 106
Phiz *see* Brown
Piccadilly, 56, 73
Pickering, ·· ·· , res, 138–9
Pigburn, Frances, murder victim, 142–4, 152, 157
Pinberry, Mr (decd), 70
Pitmilly, L.J., 126
Playhouse Yard, 160
Pleasance, Scotland, 117, 123, 127
Plumstead churchyard, 70, 171
Plymouth, 64, 78
Pople, Richard, con, 81
Portsea, 78
Portsmouth Street, 61
Portugal Street, 146
Potterow, Edinburgh, 18, 92
Powell, Henry and John, bereaved anti-
  resurrectionists, 75
Prince, John, assistant watchman, 73–4
Prince Regent, the, 55

Quakers, 20
Queen Anne, 4
Queen Caroline, 5

Rae, Sir William, advocate, 125–6, 127, 128
'Rag Fair' (Rosemary Lane street
  market), 160, 163
Red Lion Court, 160
Reigate, 65
Rey, William, convicted felon, 5
Richardson, ·· ·· , res, 18
Robinson, Sam, prizefighter, 37
Rose, ·· ·· , watchman, 71
Ross, Eliza (Mrs Edward Cook),
  murderess, 159–68
Rosyth, 92, 96
Roughead, William, crime historian, 104
Royal College of Surgeons, 5, 13, 32, 34, 35, 43, 63, 69, 169
Royal Hospital, Hampshire, 78
Russell, Dr, 21
Rymer's gin-shop, 116, 117

Sacheverall, Revd Dr, 11
Sadler, John, MP, 137
Sainsbury, Mrs Jane (decd), 10
St Albans, 55–6, 90
St Albans, Duchess of, 71
St Andrew's burial ground, Holborn, 77
St Andrew's church, Holborn, 10, 11, 77–8
St Bartholmew's church, Smithfield, 77
St Bartholmew's Hospital, 10, 13, 33, 37, 40, 43, 46, 47, 48, 49, 84, 144, 148, 149
St Botolph's churchyard, 76
St Clement Danes' burial ground, 146
St Clement Danes' workhouse, 136
St Dunstan's burial ground, 61
St George's churchyard, Bloomsbury, 10
St George's Fields, 145
St George's Fields' House of
  Correction, 12
St George's Hospital, 7, 10, 33, 34, 40, 48, 8
St George's-in-the-East, 79
St Giles's parish, 49, 64, 130
St Helen's church, Bishopsgate, 77
St James's church, Clerkenwell, 43, 70
St John's chapel, Walworth, 139
St Katharine's Dock, 163
St Leonard's church, Shoreditch, 142
St Leonard's churchyard, Shoreditch, 72
St Mary Axe, 35, 36
St Pancras, 49, 135
St Pancras burying ground, 50, 51

St Pancras Hospital, 34
St Paul's Churchyard, 135
St Peter's church, Cornhill, 77
St Saviour's churchyard, 10, 62
St Sepulchre's church, 32
St Thomas's Hospital, 10, 33, 35, 46, 47, 48, 52–3, 59, 61, 62, 63, 65, 66, 67–8, 76, 84, 144, 171
Sampson, Agnes, witch, 17
Sampson and Lion public house, Shadwell, 160
Samuel, ···, res, 18
Sarre, France, 41
Scotland, 13, 14–20, 28, 29, 33, 88, 89–103, 132–4, 136–7
Scottish Mercury, The, 31
Scottish Royal College of Physicians, 134
Scottish Royal College of Surgeons, 134
'Screw, The', res, 92
Seager, John, watchman, 73–4, 75
Seager, Joseph, s. to above, 73
Select Committee on the Teaching of Anatomy, 45, 81–8
Shoreditch, 72, 140, 143, 145, 146
Shoreditch High Street, 142, 147
Shearman, John alias Shearing, res, 70, 71, 81, 86
Sheldon, Thomas, s/a, 9
Sheepscar, Leeds, 138
Shields, Michael, por, 144, 149, 150, 153, 154
Sibthorp, Col., MP, 170
Simpson, Abigail, murder victim, 108
Simpson, Miss, d. to above, 108, 116
Smith, Bill, res, 71, 74
Smith, John Southwood, s/a, 69, 144
Smithfield, 135, 148, 160
Soho, 34, 139
South Africa, 96
South, John Flintwood, s/a, 34, 40–1, 44, 47, 62, 79, 144
Southwark, 12, 36, 49, 59, 62, 67, 149, 160
Sparrer, Mr, stu, 52–3
Spitalfields gang, the, 69–72, 86
Spittal churchyard, Aberdeen, 19
'spoiling', 39, 85
'Spune, The', res, 100, 101, 102, 103, 133
Star Inn, Portsea, 78
Stirling, 105
Stonielaw's Close, Edinburgh, 24, 26, 27–8, 31
Stony Stratford, 136
Strichan, L.J., 29
Suny, Sarah (decd), 12
Surgeons' College, Edinburgh, 15
Surgeons' Hall, 4, 5, 9

Surgeon's Square, Edinburgh, 15, 16, 17, 90, 97, 101, 111, 112, 115, 125, 130
Surrey Assizes, 74
Sutton, ··· (?Hutton), con, 71
Sutton, Henry, prizefighter, 37
Swanston, William, publican, 109
Swanston's rumshop, 109
Syme, Henry, s/a, 97, 120, 130, 133

Tait, George, Sheriff Substitute, 108
Tanner's Close, Edinburgh, 106, 112, 115, 118
Tenterden, Lord, 137
Thavies Inn, 10
Thomas, John, res, 70
Thomas, Superintendent, 151, 152, 153, 154
Thomson, Mowbray, s/a and res, 90–1
Thomas, Mr, cutler, 51
'Tim Tickler', pseudonymous conversationalist, 113–14
Times, The, 9, 50, 52–3, 58, 78, 136
Tinwald, Lord Justice-Clerk, 29, 30
Tobacco Lane, Leeds, 138
Tolbooth Prison, Edinburgh, 28
Tomlinson, Richard, res, 70
'toothing', 35–6, 41, 53, 56
Torrence, Helen, murderess, 21–31
Tower of London menagerie, 35
Tower Hill, 56
Trainer, Tom, boy, 147–8
Trueby, Mr and Mrs John, landlords of Bishop and Head, 140, 156
Turner, Ned, prizefighter, 75
Tuson, Mr, s/a, 147
Tyburn, 8
Tyrone, 104

Union Canal, 105
Union Hall magistrates' office, 59, 70
United Borough Hospitals, 10, 13, 37, 40, 62, 67
Uxbridge, 71

Vaizey, Sarah, suspected murder victim, 166
Vaughan, Sir John, J., 154, 156
Vaughan, ···, res, 60, 61, 63–4, 67, 78, 81, 86
Virginia Road, 147

Wakley, Thomas, medical journalist, 63, 68, 82
Waldie, Jean, murderess, 21–31
Wallis, Thomas, res, 59–61
Walmsgate, York, 134–5
Walsh, Caroline, match-seller, 160–7

Walsh, Catherine, lame pauper, 165
Walter, Bill, sportsman, 75
Walworth, 139
Warburton, Henry, MP, 81, 83, 137, 169, 171, 172
Warrington, 80, 132
Waterloo, battle of, 53, 96
Watkins, Thomas, res, 70–2
    see also John Head, Thomas Williams
Watling Street, 37
Webb Street, 62, 148, 149
Weeks, ·· ··, por, 148
Weill, Dr Levy, murderer, 9
Wellington, Duke of, 41
West, Benjamin, RA, 34
Westkirk, 18
Westminster Hospital, 10, 33, 40, 84
West Port (or Wester Port or Portsburgh), 106, 111, 113, 115, 129
Whackett, ·· ··, cemetery keeper, 60, 73
White, ·· ··, res, 43, 102
Whitechapel, 139, 160, 162
White Horse Cellar, 70
Whitehead, ·· ··, pitch-plaster victim, 134–5
Whitehead, Mrs, m. to above, 134
Wight, ·· ··, res, 102, 124
Wild, Jonathan, 4–5, 9
Wildes, ?'Patrick', res, 44, 59, 60, 61, 64–5, 67, 81, 82, 86, 171

Wildes, Mrs, w. to above, 64–5
Williams, Mr, stu, 52–3
Williams, Peter, res, 10
Williams, Revd Theodore, 156–7, 158
Williams, Thomas see Watkins and Head
Williamson, Andrew, con, 111
Wilson, 'Daft Jamie', 115–16, 123–4, 125, 126
Wilson, James, s/a, 33, 46
Wilson, John, 'Christopher North', journalist, 109, 113–14, 128, 130
Wilson, Miss, of Bruntsfield Links, 92
Wilson, Mrs and Miss, n-o-k to Daft Jamie, 115, 117, 129, 130
Wimbledon, 41
Windmill Street see Great Windmill Street
Wontner, Governor, of Newgate, 156
Wood Street, 36
Woods, Michael, or John, res, 60, 61, 65, 75
Worship Street magistrates' office, 36
Worthington, Mrs, probable procuress, 109, 110, 111, 117
Wortley, ·· ··, con, 59, 70
Wych Street, 32, 36

Yarmouth, 63, 78
York, 134–5